Decorative Woodcarving

The Complete Course

GRAHAM R. BULL

STERLING PUBLISHING CO., INC.
New York

FROM LIGHT TO SHADOW,
BEHOLDER'S EYES
BECKON MORE FROM THE
HAND OF THE MAKER.

To my mother, Thirza, who, watching her teenage son
sitting on the laundry step, idly whittling a stick, suggested
it would be better if I did something more useful with it.

Library of Congress Cataloging-in-Publication Data
Bull, Graham R.
  Decorative woodcarving : the complete course / Graham R. Bull.
    p. cm.
  Includes index.
  ISBN 0-8069-9587-4
  1. Wood-carving. I. Title.
TT199.7.B85 2000
736'.4—dc21   99-43498
                                            CIP

Designed by Judy Morgan
Edited by Rodman P. Neumann

1 3 5 7 9 10 8 6 4 2
Published by Sterling Publishing Company, Inc.
387 Park Avenue South, New York, N.Y. 10016
© 2000 by Graham R. Bull
Distributed in Canada by Sterling Publishing
c/o Canadian Manda Group, One Atlantic Avenue, Suite 105
Toronto, Ontario, Canada M6K 3E7
Distributed in Great Britain and Europe by Cassell PLC
Wellington House, 125 Strand, London WC2R 0BB, England
Distributed in Australia by Capricorn Link (Australia) Pty Ltd.
P.O. Box 6651, Baulkham Hills, Business Centre, NSW 2153, Australia
Printed in China
Sterling ISBN 0-8069-9587-4

CONTENTS

PREFACE

Decorative Woodcarving: The Complete Course is based on two woodcarving courses, "Decorative Woodcarving" Levels II and III, which were designed in 1995 and received accreditation in Australia in January 1997 from the New South Wales Vocational Education Training Accreditation Board. The courses are recognized throughout Australia, and are unique in that country.

During 1997 and 1998, the students' work was recorded in a series of photographs that documented their learning process, from their very first attempt to their last graduation piece. Selected photographs are used in the text to illustrate not only the right way, but also the things that can go wrong. You will see a real-life study of the learning of the craft of relief woodcarving, covering the challenges that any novice woodcarver would experience.

The courses were designed and taught by Graham Bull, self-taught from teenage years after facing the frustration of the refusal of local professional carvers to give away their "trade secrets." Teaching about 150 students a year at his Whistlewood Studio in Sydney, these very secrets are now his curriculum for students as young as six.

Each chapter discusses a different aspect of the learning of the craft, and throughout the text there are many hints, tips, and explanations that will ensure your own learning process is made much easier. Equally, anyone not specifically interested in woodcarving but more in art generally will find fascinating reading within the pages.

Acknowledgments

For contributing so willingly and submitting their every mistake to the camera for the world to see, a rare group of students: Gerald Bohun, Peter Clarke, Stuart Edgecombe-Walker, David Gunn, Theo Kennis, Donald McKerrell, Pauline Nolan, Stan Smith and Anne Waining. Also for their many barbecues over two years of course work.

For the gift of my first real woodcarving chisels on my twenty-first birthday, thirty-one years ago, from my wife, Nancy.

For access to special historical exhibits mentioned within the text: Judith Buist for Frederick Tod carvings and drawings; the Very Reverend Keith Jones, Dean of St. Peter's Cathedral of Exeter, for the "Exeter Elephant" brochure photograph; the Sydney Power House Museum for photography of Frederick Tod's eagle lectern drawing; the Reverend Gim Pettigrew, Rector of St. John's of Gordon, Sydney, for Frederick Tod's eagle lectern; Mr. Donald McKerrel for photography from Lanoch Castle in New Zealand; Ms. Vanessa Rowed and Malcolm Paisley for their hands; Mr. Bill Shean for the Gidgee bird carving; Mr. Andrew Tarlington for the Terrace carving; and Mr. Jim Anderson for various line drawings.

For strong support contributing to the establishment of the accredited courses, and the promotion of them: Mr. Richard Stokes, Director, the NSW Furnishings Industry Training Council; Mr. Les Miller, Course Examiner and Woodwork Educationalist; Mr. Rex Swinton, Principal (now retired), Chatswood Evening College, Sydney; and all the staff at the *Australian Woodworker* and *House and Home* magazines.

For course administration, desktop publishing, and word processing, Linda Lubica Srank.

chapter 1

IN THE BEGINNING

Your New Journey

Once a way of life, decorative woodcarving is now mostly a pastime. For many, a pastime is a way of life. For others it is just one of life's pleasures, and for some a potential new profession. Whichever is the case for you, woodcarving remains one of the most ancient of the arts and continues to fascinate even the most distant of participants.

I wrote this book especially for the two kinds of potential woodcarver that make up the vast majority. You have either never thought about the prospect of taking on wood-carving, or have thought about it very briefly and have rejected the idea, because you decided that you just couldn't do it.

Like most art forms, a certain amount of skill is needed to effectively execute the creative process. In the following chapters, the participant will be taken along the path towards the successful learning of these skills.

The learning process can often be confusing and frustratingly slow, and one of the major reasons for this is that more often than not the student learning from a book is told what to do, but not enough of what not to do. As a result, the student ends up doing mostly what not to do, and when we see it "not going right" we conclude we can't do it properly. Then disappointment and, worst of all, disillusionment, take over.

What happens generally is that we don't go "far" enough in our carving. So it never looks right. We stop before we get there, so to speak. Through these pages, there is a lot of the "what not to do."

For this reason, words are kept to the point, photographs are used to show both good and not so good, and you will be able to follow through and do for yourself from the simplest of carvings to some more complex work that you never thought possible.

Just think what your friends will say when you tell them, "I'm doing woodcarving!" They will be intrigued, fascinated, and curious. After all, woodcarving is a fairly unusual thing to be doing in this day and age. But once you get into it, you will wonder just why you weren't doing it all along!

Another reason for sometimes "too slow" a learning curve is that we may be so intent on trying to follow the written word that our approach becomes clouded in dogma. That is, we get caught in a the-book-said-I-must-do-it-this-way approach. If the particular way of going about carving doesn't suit us for whatever reason, then we lose impetus. Throughout this book, therefore, there is a constant reference to the what-works-for-you approach, not only in the way things are done, but also in terms of what is done. If you are unhappy with the end result, and unless it was meant to be a reproduction of someone else's work, then is there much point in doing it a certain way to get an unhappy conclusion? Of course not!

A Little Bit of History

No one knows when the first woodcarving was created. Maybe it was when the first wooden club was invented—or maybe it was the first spear tip. What we do know is that carving wood and stone and anything else has been around for tens of thousands of years, and that some very famous people were woodcarvers: people like Jesus of Nazareth, Abraham Lincoln, Michelangelo, and Neolithic Man, just to name a few.

Some of the best known individuals who were famous as woodcarvers include Tilmann Riemanschneider (Germany, 1460–1531), Grinling Gibbons (England, 1648, in Holland to 1721), and Jacobo Tatti (Italy, 1486–1570). The English learned to carve from the Germans; the Egyptians did it 3,500 years ago; Polynesians, Australian aborigines, the Chinese, and the Mesopotamians did it long before that.

Carving has been used by man to decorate everything and anything—weapons, boats, carriages, walls, picture frames, staircases, roof beams, boxes, light fittings, spoons, shoes, pulpits, walking sticks, toothpicks, doors, bed headboards and footboards, combs, coffins, gable ends. You name it; we've done it! The woodcarving that seems to stand out as the most commonly enduring to this day is the decoration of furniture. If today's woodcarver couldn't (or wouldn't) decorate furniture, then there wouldn't be too much food on his or her table.

Like most things, carving has had its ups and downs. Commonplace during the time of Christ and for a couple hundred years more, carving then fell into a recession for another five or six hundred years, except in places like India, China, Persia, and Asia Minor. The Scandinavians led a revival in the ninth century, and by the eleventh century carving was again commonplace throughout Europe. It peaked again during the eighteenth century; then the age of the machine took over, and carving just about disappeared as a commercial proposition (except for furniture). Since Victorian days, there just hasn't been much woodcarving at all.

Ironically, one of the results of the emergence of the age of technology has been a ripple of interest once again in the craft of carving. This is partially a result of ever-increasing amounts of leisure time brought on by automation. It is also because people want to try to make a living from it, particularly as a "value added" part of furniture making and antiques restoration. Decorative carvings are also a popular tourist souvenir in Asia and parts of Africa.

It is appropriate to note that woodcarving has been known historically not as an art or craft, but as a trade. Could it be that the technology that killed the trade may be the technology that produced the craft? Another couple of hundred years and we will have the answer.

Woodcarving, however, is essentially an art form, like painting, photography, and cake decorating. As such, there is great subjectivity as to the viewer's likes and dislikes regarding the end result. And the moment something is subjective, there are as many right answers as there are people reviewing the end work. It is true that certain characteristics help place designs in a time period, or with a certain maker, or from a particular country or region. And to be nothing other than perfectly reasonable, these characteristics must be present if the work is to be described as being "of" a particular style. But never be mistaken—a period of time is just that. It is not and cannot be finite. In art, things change with time. So the Jacobean detail at the beginning (if that can actually be pinpointed) of the Jacobean period will be different from that of the end—whenever that actually was!

So when we look at period examples, we should avoid being dogmatic, but rather encourage experimentation in their interpretation.

Not a great deal is known about many individual carvers. Because they were tradesmen, they tended to follow the work and moved around considerably, even from country to country. They often worked in groups on one project, and accordingly there are very few records of who actually did what. A carver would often subcontract work or hire apprentices or tradesmen of different skill levels, and some carvings reflect these different skill levels by having good, bad, or indifferent work in the one piece.

To add to the anonymous nature of things, carvers were unusual in that they were not generally known to seek personal recognition for their work. Provided they got their pay and they could be on their way, they were happy. Work was all very much a team effort and this was probably just as well, judging by some of the monumental works that are to be found in old buildings and museums. However, the individual certainly left his mark, judging by the individuality to be found in abundance in cathedrals throughout the world.

During the fourteenth century, the stone mason was often also a woodcarver. Often demand outstripped supply, so that master designs were carved in wood and plaster casts were taken to enable multiple production of ornamentation such as the architectural decoration of ceiling cornices and roses.

Nobility throughout the world very frequently commissioned decorative work for their castles, churches, and palaces. Commissioned works also became gifts from the nobility of one country to another. International influences can be seen in many carvings that still exist today. For example, a winged ornamentation typical of an Egyptian carving or a tenth-century Islamic design might be present in an eleventh-century church carving in England.

Up to about the tenth century, woodcarvers didn't appear to have a particularly good grasp of the nature of wood as a medium with which to work. As a result, a lot of their efforts ended up splitting rather badly, and in many areas literally falling apart as the wood seasoned. At one time there was apparently quite a business to be had in the restoration of carvings that had fallen apart. This was also a problem with shipbuilding at the time, with unseasoned woods shrinking or twisting so that often the ships sank before they were commissioned. Hopefully the woodcarver had been paid for the production of the figureheads and transoms before nature took over!

As always, history books are full of all sorts of snippets of interest, and there is no chance that we are going to do justice to history here. But do remember that when you take up the ancient trade, and become a part of the creation of a modern craft, you will be adding your snippet to the history of art. And so that future historians will know who did what, please sign each piece, even if it's just so that your great-grandchildren will know of the contributions you have made.

Wood, Your Most Important Carving Partner

Timeless, versatile, sometimes demanding and fickle—and not always forgiving—whether you carve it or just look at it, wood is a most extraordinary material. From one tree comes wood in different colors, strengths, grain patterns, perfumes, ages, densities, and workability. Wood can tell you how old it is, and what weather it has had to put up with during its life as a tree. If you don't understand wood, it can frustrate you. But once you get to know it, the wood will tell you whether you can carve it, what you can make with it, and what you can't do with it.

Your piece of wood has come from a tree that has been a vital part of man's survival, not the least because it has helped remove toxic carbon monoxide from the air and helped to produce life-giving oxygen. The roots of the tree have helped to hold the soil together and stop erosion by wind and rain, and the discarded leaves have helped to enrich the soil's ability to give life to other plants.

Your piece of wood is an amazing array of layers of cells that carried water and other nutrients from the ground, stored food made by the leaves so that more wood could grow, and supported the branches that carried the leaves that made it all happen.

Your piece of wood will stir in you all kinds of different emotions. You will use your senses of touch, sight, smell, and hearing. You will be inquisitive, sometimes impatient. You will achieve and be happy, and make some mistakes and be sad. You will nearly always be relaxed, sometimes excited, and rarely anxious. As you create, you will make decisions that you've never made before, thought you never could make, and may never make again. You will never forget your experience.

Pick up your piece of wood, and even with no knowledge of what species it is, you will immediately sense its texture, its weight, its color, its smell, its hardness, its age. You will soon form an opinion as to whether you like it and whether you would like to make something from it, and you will soon start to wonder just what.

Wood is most remarkable when you think of the incredible number of things we do with it. We admire its beauty; it keeps us warm; we sit on it, sit at it, eat off it, sleep on it, and live under it. And now you're about to start carving into it!

Your piece of wood will become your close and most important carving partner—no two pieces being the same. Learn from what it tells you, handle each piece with care and respect, and you will experience the joy and satisfaction of creating your very first carving.

The Tools for Your Art

Most of us at one time or another have handled handyman tools, even if simply the trusty hammer or screwdriver. Maybe you can remember the scroll saw in woodwork or the hacksaw in metalwork at school? For some of us it may be the rusty pruning saw or the blunt pruning shears in the garden.

Chisels and mallets, then, might just be a bit of a worry. Not to mention clamps and dividers and oilstones and strops and polishing wax!

Before panic sets in, let's take a look at five points that will cheer you up:

※ First, none of the tools you will really need have any moving parts; they are very simple.

※ Because they are very simple, it is very easy to understand what each one does. To be able to use them effectively requires only practice.

※ The simplicity of the tools means that they have fairly broadly defined tasks, which in turn means that you don't have to make too many management decisions. If you consider that a tool becomes nothing more that an extension of your hand, then all you have to do is get your brain to tell your hand what to do, and vice versa, and you've got it made—well, almost!

※ Always remember that there is no substitute for quality. The quality of your tools will definitely have a major influence on the degree of ease that you will encounter, and will show in the appearance of the end results of your work; we will look at this in the next few pages. We will also take a look at how to recognize "good" and "poor" quality tools.

※ Last, looking after your newly acquired tools is very easy and very essential—you can't carve with a blunt and rusty chisel. The routine of managing your tools will soon become second nature to you.

Designs and Ideas for Wood Carving

Perhaps one of the greatest perceived problems we face is the search for carving material. "Perceived" is the key word, because quite simply there is so much material as to make an endless supply for everyone's lifetime. Once we realize why we carve, then we are off to a good start to select the most appropriate material for us as individuals.

1-1. Fluorescent lighting produces unrealistic color and a shadowless environment and makes details very difficult to see.

What Can I Carve?

We have said carving is an art form. As such, then, its primary role is to decorate. Either to decorate the piece of wood itself, as a part of a larger object such as an item of furniture, or to assist in the overall decoration of an environment, such as a wall plaque for the kitchen.

We carve, then, to decorate an otherwise uninteresting surface. "Uninteresting" of course is defined in the eye of the beholder, so this in itself will temper our carving requirements. If we compare the individual as carver to an artist painting a picture, we soon find ourselves in a position where, if the painters has millions of colors to choose from, we have only the color of the wood and the shadows we put into it. In essence, unless we use multi-colored wood—such as highly figured camphor tree with its reds, browns, greens, yellows, and everything in between—we have only two colors; the wood and the shadow.

1-2. An unshaded regular household light bulb produces truer color, and more detail is visible because some shadow is being formed.

It is the shadows that we create that make the woodcarving we see. The creation of shadows is the most important "paint" for the woodcarver. Relief carving is all about shadows. Think relief, think shadow. Shadow intensity can be varied, and this you will achieve with experimentation. Shadow can be used to "tell the lies" of perspective. Shadows create the illusions of depth, distance, and shape. Shadows cleverly created will give the illusion of things existing when they don't exist at all. The creation of shadow requires the existence of light. And herein is the secret to successful relief carving.

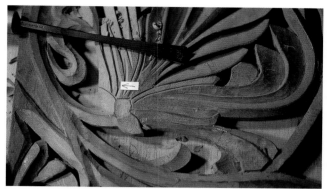

1-3. Shade the bulb to direct the light; move it to one side of the carving to create shadows that make everything very visible.

About Light

The light by which we carve will dictate how well we see what we are actually doing, and the light that falls on our finished carving will determine the visual qualities of the end result. This cannot be overstated, and must be experimented with over and over again.

The following will set the scene for all our shadow discussions that follow:

At first, we need to discuss the light by which we do our carving. A relief pattern directly below a fluorescent tube is shown in 1-1. The color is not realistic and the carving is generally featureless.

Fluorescent lights are designed to diffuse the light they transmit in a nonshadow-forming manner. They are designed for work environments, where shadow is *not* wanted—as in an office where there is a lot of paper work. They are low users of power (used where price is a major consideration). The detail of the carving in 1-1 is very difficult to see.

The view in 1-2 is taken directly underneath an unshaded regular filament household lightbulb. The direct light tends to concentrate the light in a far more coherent fashion. The colors are also truer. Much more of the detail is visible, because there are shadows being formed, unlike in 1-1. A household lightbulb is a more direct form of lighting.

The view in 1-3 is the same again, except it is taken with the same light shaded and moved to one side of the carving (in this case to the left). Note how the density of the shadows increases, considerably enhancing the visibility of the features of the carved surface. In fact, the carving error indicated by the arrow in the center of the carving is not at all visible in 1-1.

Avoid Flourescent Light

Never use fluorescent lighting for your woodcarving, because it is essentially a "shadowless" light and literally hides the very things you want to see. In fact it is very difficult to see what you are doing at all. A wall-mounted or desktop reading lamp creates ideal shadows for carving.

The Creation of Shadow

The simple theory of the creation of shadow is shown in 1-4 to 1-8. When light shines onto a flat uncarved surface, as shown in 1-4, no shadows are formed. The light is reflected off the surface with no other visual effect being formed.

The same light beam is reflected off a carved surface in 1-5. A shadow is formed in the area between the line of the light beam and the edge of the carving. In 1-6, we can see that varying strengths of shad-

ow can be formed depending on the degree to which the wood is cut first in the vertical plane, and then undercut to create a "cavern" that causes a much darker shadow to be formed in that area.

Another concept to be grasped is that in most circumstances, a convex curve will cause less shadow effects to be formed than will a concave curve. This is shown in 1-7 and 1-8, where we can clearly see the effects of surface curve and shadow formation.

What Light Shows

In the end, then, we can see that the light by which we carve shows us more or less clearly what we are doing, and the light illuminating the end result shows us what we have done.

And What about You?

Of all the people in the world, this book is intended for you. This book is not the summation of one person's bidding on the world for woodcarving, but rather a discussion of the opinions of a teacher, and the results of the student. Neither one is right or wrong, nor rarely will they "meet in the middle." Probably just as well! The majority of the pictorial content of this book is of the work of a teacher and the students who followed the teacher's guidance in learning the skills. Their results are a consequence of their interaction with one another, the teacher, and their own aspirations.

This is not gospel to an individual. It is a story of several individuals' self-development. It is of their

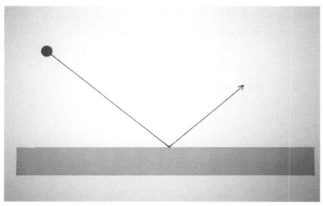

1-4. A flat surface creates no shadow.

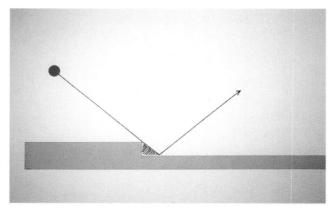

1-5. The edge of the carving together with the directed light beam allows a shadow to be formed.

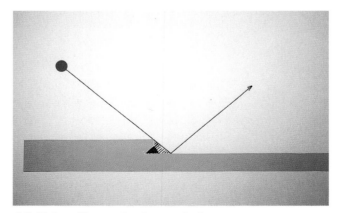

1-6. Undercutting creates stronger shadows.

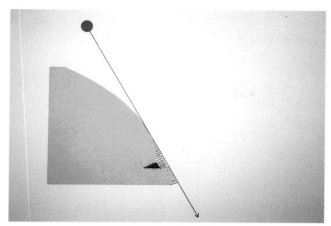

1-7. Convex curves generally produce fewer shadows.

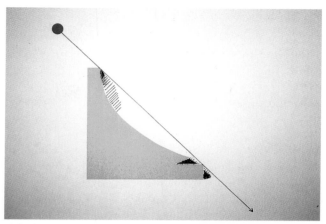

1-8. Concave curves generally allow more opportunities for the creation of shadows.

work as they move through their individual learning processes. There are some examples of the teacher's work, but this is a book for the people by the people, literally. It is a book of a learning curve by a group of people who had never before in their lives done any woodcarving. Two or three of the contributors had only ever done hobby woodworking, and each had done a little at school. But woodcarving, never.

Decorative Woodcarving: The Complete Course is a testament to the degree of accomplishment and dexterity the "manually average" potential woodcarving student can develop and display with a degree of perseverance for the learning of this manual skill. With a degree of practice, the new woodcarver can become quite a maverick.

With luck, and application, this might just be you.

chapter 2

WHICH TOOL?

*Making
Right
Choices
Takes Time*

Does chisel balance matter? How do you stop your tools from going rusty? Is there really anything wrong with soft steel? What is wrong with hard steel? Is there anything to be concerned about when buying secondhand chisels? What sort of mallet should you use? Why? What kind of workbench is "ideal" and what sort of vise should you get? Yes, there are as many questions as there are tools. Let's see if we can sort it all out.

The "right" tool will depend on the individual as much as the application, and for that reason tools should be purchased as they are needed rather than in advance. Rather than spend a considerable amount of money up front to find that it is misspent, if it need have been spent at all, it is best for the carver to progressively find his or her comfort zone.

For the woodworker, one of the greatest addictions of all is not simply the urge of doing it, but rather the desire to have the very thing needed to do it with—hand tools. We always seem to be able to invent a need for a new one, no matter how many we already have! Unfortunately, when you start out, tools are also the very things that confuse you the most. Your first gouge, mallet, or slipstone can be the most confusing purchase of all. There are so many unknowns, there is so much to think about, and quite often the price is enough to make us so wary of making a mistake that we tread timidly and become quite nervous about it all.

Often solely the salesman guides us—and we soon discover that the salesmen aren't always all that knowledgeable either—a bit like "the blind leading the blind." "You will need a set of these . . ." is the most common phrase of the salesman to maximize his sale and minimize what is left in your pocket! And that will become our first "tool rule"—never buy a set of anything, unless you know for sure it is exactly what you want. Always buy your tools individually, as and when you need them. We will discuss this in greater depth later.

Each of our tool purchases should add to the pleasure of our activities, by making our work easier and more comfortable to complete. And this forms the basis of our second "tool rule"—the "right" tool is the one that best fits our "comfort zone." If you aren't comfortable with it, then don't buy it. A little later we will see that our comfort zone is very much a personal thing, cannot be dictated to us, and will depend entirely on our individual preferences—the point being that what is good for one person may be quite unsatisfactory for another. This is another reason for not rushing into a flurry of tool buying.

So there is our starting point—two tool rules to get us going.

⚔ Don't buy sets of tools predetermined by somebody other than yourself, and

⚔ Make sure each purchase is within your personal comfort zone.

With these rules in mind, let's move on and take a look at the various tools we will need to learn about, and how we might go about deciding which ones to buy:

The most important tools, of course, are mallets and chisels, sharpening stones and strops, and light. Let's examine them one at a time.

The Mallet

The mallet was invented to fulfill an inability of the hand to satisfactorily push a chisel through wood. Let's examine this more closely, and then look at what design it should be.

These SIDE BOXES will look at the implications of many of the things we ignore or take for granted, as well as some of the things we decide "can't be done," when, in reality, they can. We will also address how to properly manage your tools

This is not about first aid, but is about being aware of things you may not think about until it is too late. Like breathing in pigments, or spontaneous combustion from linseed oil. Or breaking a lightbulb with your chisel and electrocuting yourself or making your carving life miserable with fluorescent lights.

But First, a Note about Our Hands

Before we take a look at tools, let's take a look at our hands. Both right and left. Let's take a look at what they are connected to, and let's see if we can get a handle on how these amazing things work. Between your neck and the tip of your middle finger there are 32 bones, plus blood vessels, muscles, nerves, fat, skin, and other tissue surrounding them all. Messages from your brain activate muscles that move bones. When you pick up a tool and your fingers wrap around its handle, a whole system of "levers" is activated. This system, in conjunction with your eyes, even weighs the tool, and measures it, and sends a message to your brain with an assessment of whether or not it believes your particular system can handle it easily, with difficulty, or indeed at all.

It doesn't matter if your hand is big, small, fat, thin, strong, weak, or arthritic. An assessment will be made and a message will get through. What *does* matter is that *every* hand will make a *different* assessment; even your own left and right ones will vary. This assessment depends not only on the characteristics of your mechanical (motor) system and how it relates physically to the tool, but also your history of previous experiences with handling tools. If you are right-handed, it will feel funny in your left hand. If you are left-handed, your right hand mightn't want to know about it. Because there is an infinite set of data that combine to make an assessment, the end result is that every one of us is different.

As is the case when we first start out on most new things, we discover that there are a lot of new experiences we need to think about from a safety point of view. We might discover that we have physical or mental limitations, or that what we thought was a good idea really isn't. There is no realistic "order of priorities" in which to address these issues, so let's look at our limitations.

Coping with Physical Impairments

Woodcarving is an activity that can be attractive to a wide variety of people who find themselves in situations of physical difficulty. For its therapeutic value, woodcarving is like any other art form, and the very nature of its creativity makes it an ideal pursuit for those who would benefit from such activities. It is surprising to me that it is not a more commonly listed activity in the areas of occupational therapy.

Woodcarving is not generally a physically demanding activity; it is certainly low impact, and can easily be done sitting down. For this reason, those who are wheelchair-bound need not find it a forbidding or difficult task, especially with relief carving. With a little imagination as to the design of a workbench to suit the accommodation of a wheelchair, it becomes a very practical, fulfilling, and worthwhile hobby or profession. The conversion of a garage is an ideal space for the wheelchair, as it has no step access and there is room to maneuver.

Conveniently placed light switches and sufficient lights on separate switches so that different lighting combinations can be easily achieved also make it quite an attractive proposition for the interested artist who is wheelchair-bound.

Woodworking has long been an activity for the blind, whether totally or partially, and woodcarving is no different. Chisel identification marks on the handles and a convenient tool rack with corresponding marks for storage are a great help. A bench with a lip around the edge to prevent tools from rolling off is easy to set up. Templates can be used to cut around for relief carving, and shape can be taught by feel as can anything else.

Our experiences will tell us that the drawing of a straight line is foreign to the operation of the mechanics of our hands and arms. This is not necessarily because our mechanics aren't capable of doing it, but because we haven't trained our brain to control our mechanics so that they operate in a straight line. The key word is *control*. If you push your carving chisel across the wood and you aren't in control, it will go in the wrong direction—you will slip, and most likely damage your carving. You may be "out of control" because, for example, your brain isn't trained enough, or your muscles aren't strong enough. Your mallet, you will discover, is a great substitute for both. Instead of holding the chisel in one hand and pushing it with the other, you can tap it in exactly the direction and to the distance you want it to go. The most important use for your mallet is *control*. The harder or softer you hit it, the more or less the chisel will move. Once you are in control, the more *power* you apply, the greater the cut. *Power* is the mallet's other reason for being.

The trick, then, is to have a mallet that helps you move the chisel both far enough and in the right direction at the same time.

You need a mallet that is the right design configuration to give the most effective combination of control and power. Your personal characteristics, the style of carving, and the wood you are working with will determine this combination of control and power.

What Shape Should Your Mallet Be?
When we are carving, we are most likely chiseling in a curve, unlike a carpenter, for example, who works mostly in straight lines. We will be using a lot of hand and wrist movement, the center of our swing mostly being from the elbow, unlike the carpenter, who will generally be swinging from the shoulder. So we need a mallet that can cope with hitting the end of our chisel accurately from any direction, unlike a carpenter, who will hit straight onto the chisel. The hitting surface of your mallet, then, must always present itself in the same way to the chisel handle, irrespective of the direction from which it comes. Basic geometry indicates that this surface is curved, and not flat. This is why a carpenter's mallet is square, and a carver's mallet is round, in cross section, and tapered longitudinally: round to cope with a twist of the wrist, and tapered (cone-shaped) to cope with the arc of the strike.

You will find that four inches (100mm) is about right for the length of the head. Too much shorter and it is too easy to miss, and too much longer will make it too cumbersome. A regular carpenter's mallet is compared to a selection of carvers' mallets in 2-1.

Make the smaller diameter near the handle about 15 percent less than the larger. There is no precise reason for this, other than that elusive element called experience.

Weight and weight distribution are next. If we want greater power, to carve a large hardwood sculpture for example, we need heavy weight delivery unrestricted by our hand and arm movements. The balance or weight distribution of the mallet when we are holding it needs to be skewed towards the head and away from the hand (the mallet needs to feel a bit top-heavy). If, on the other hand, it is great control we want, the weight needs to be less, and the balance needs to be closer to our hand, which is controlling the mallet's movements. A top-heavy mallet will be a hindrance to achieving maximum control.

Mallet weight is determined by the amount and kind of material that is used in making it. So if it is turned from wood (the most common), select the density (weight per unit volume) to suit the purpose. High density for heavier mallets, lower for lighter. Through continued use a wooden mallet will eventually break up, so consideration needs to be given to the impact resistance of the wood. In Australia, for example, "good" woods are tallowwood, jarrah, weeping myall, and purpleheart; in Europe or North America try beech, oak, apple, or pear wood; and in North America try box, dogwood, or hickory.

Each and all of the potential threats to your well-being addressed in these side boxes will be relevant to you at some time or other during your carving career.

With regard to any of the subject matter that is, or is potentially, of a medical nature, it is always best to consult your medical doctor. None of the comments within these side boxes are by any means exhaustive, and they are here specifically and only to highlight the need to be aware of possible hazards.

Accidents Can Happen to You, Too

Safety is not the realm of the other person. It *can* happen to you. Safety is about yourself and your environment and what you can achieve in what might seem to be adversity, such as suffering the restriction of arthritis when using mallets.

Some of the most obvious accidents with woodcarving are the occasional cuts that occur, mainly as a result of carelessness. Unfortunately, this also represents one of the greatest sources of threat to the carver with the possibility of diseases being introduced to the blood.

The whole ergonomics of carving is also important for your safety. Your posture, the workbench you are using, its height, and your ease of working around it are important. So is the seat you are using, and the hardness of the floor. They all combine to create comfortable, stress-free, and injury-free work.

2-1. A square-headed carpenter's mallet is inappropriate for a carver, who will find it easier with a round, tapered mallet head. The mallet is used for both control and power.

Injury and Mallets

Conditions such as repetitive strain injury (RSI) and "tennis elbow" may be introduced or worsened by the use of the wrong kind of mallet. A mallet that is too heavy for your personal characteristics will place unnecessary strain on your system, and one that is too light for what you are trying to achieve will cause you to hit it too hard, and could also cause painful injury.

The most important cause of stress-related injury is the relationship between the mallet's weight and weight distribution and the wood you are using. For example, the "palm mallet" (shown in 2-4 and 2-5) combined with a very soft wood like jelutong lets an arthritis sufferer carve very successfully. If you start to feel chronic pain in your wrist or any part of your arm, be careful to check these elements as well as check with your doctor. Mallet balance is very important—a top-heavy mallet can put unnecessary strain on your system, and one that is too heavy is just as damaging. One that is too light can cause you to be constantly "pushing" to get it to work for you, and this too is inappropriate.

Your work area and way of working combine with the weight and weight distribution of your mallet and the very wood you are carving to create the conditions for comfortable, stress-free, and injury-free work.

The density will help determine the general size of the mallet, but you must remember that the diameter of the handle will largely depend on the size and strength of your hand. (Ask any golfer about golf club hand grips . . .) So, the greatest flexibility for weight is in the head itself. There is nothing more uncomfortable than trying to hold on to a handle that is too thick for your hand—and it is surprising how much difference just a fraction of an inch (a millimeter or two) can make!

So it is best to get the handle right and adjust the weight of the head, by altering its diameter and/or its length. You could also use a combination of different-density woods for the head and the handle to find the correct balance.

So we need to get the right combination of your personal characteristics, the curved and tapered shape of the mallet head, and its weight and balance for the activity you wish to undertake.

While there are infinite combinations, let's pick just four of the most common requirements:

1 I have a small hand, no great strength, and want to do fine relief carving for furniture or boxes.

Try a mallet weighing 14 to 16 oz (400 to 450g), and having a center of balance as close to your hand as possible. To help achieve this, make a hollow for your thumb and index finger close to the head. The head will be about 3¼ in (85mm) long, with a diameter tapering from 2¼ in to 2 in (60mm to 50mm) and a handle about 4 in (100mm) long and 1⅛ in (28mm) thick (see 2-2).

2-2. For finer carving, the closer the center of balance is to your hand the better.

2-3. A bead helps push your hand away from the head, giving better weight distribution for heavy-duty work.

2 I am a fairly robust person who wants to do medium to large carving in the round and some garden sculpture.

Try a mallet weighing about 1 lb 5 oz to 1 lb 7 oz (600 to 650g), with a center of balance head-heavy. To help achieve this, put a bead on the handle about ⅞ in (20mm) from the head, and place your thumb and index finger on the handle side of it (see 2-3). The head will be about 4⅜ in (110mm) long, tapering from 3½ to 3 in (90 to 75mm), and the handle about 6 in (150mm) long and about 1⅜ in (35mm) thick. For extra life, less jarring, and quieter use, you may wish to use a polyurethane-headed mallet, like the one on the far right of 2-1, which does not have the bead and would be for regular use.

3 I have arthritis, and have great difficulty in holding on to a handle. I like to do wall panels and some carving in the round.

Your mallet probably won't have a traditional handle at all. Rather, it will fit in the palm of your hand, and will be a diameter that makes it easy for you to fit it in your hand without the need to firmly grip it (see 2-4). It will still be round and tapered. It will weigh 5¼ to 7 oz (150 to 200g) and, depending on your hand size, it will be about 4 in (100mm) long and its widest diameter about 2¼ in (60mm), tapering to 1 in (25mm). For extra comfort, make a hollow for your little finger (see 2-5). You are not looking for power so you should use your palm mallet in conjunction with finer chisels and softer wood such as jelutong. Consult your doctor if you have any doubts.

Diseases Introduced by Blood

Some of the most obvious accidents with wood-carving are the occasional cuts that occur, mainly as a result of carelessness. Unfortunately, these wounds also represent one of the greatest sources of threat to the woodcarver, particularly if other people are involved. Blood-transmitted diseases such as AIDS and hepatitis B cannot be cured, and can be lethal. There is no current immunization against either, and it is recommended that anyone associated with teaching woodworking or woodcarving and likely to be administering first aid be formally trained in methods to avoid blood contact.

There are some essential things you can do to protect yourself, such as wearing protective gloves while treating someone else's wound—certainly if there is no way of avoiding contact. If you are likely to do any staining or serious polishing, you will most likely have disposable rubber gloves handy in the workshop, and they should also be kept in the first-aid kit. Avoid wearing dirty gloves and therefore the potential of introducing infection to the patient. Immediately wash off any blood that gets on your skin and keep your own cuts and abrasions covered so that they will not be a source of entry for cross-infection. Immunization against hepatitis C and tetanus is highly recommended.

2-4. If you have arthritis, a palm mallet that fits comfortably in your hand may be to your advantage.

2-5. Wrap your little finger around the stubby "handle" of the palm mallet for a comfortable grip.

2-6. A "square-on" striking posture will give best results.

The Chisel, Its Handle, and Holding It

Before we look at the chisel itself, it is appropriate to look at the handle that is on it. As with mallets, the chisel handle may have a major influence on the ease with which we carve. This is the "comfort zone" I spoke of at the beginning of this chapter.

There are a number of things to take into consideration when trying to determine the best handle to use. The design of the carving and the wood we are using may dictate the kind of mallet we need. There will be certain physical design characteristics of the chisel that may influence the best handle choice. There is the action that we want to perform with the chisel, there is the kind of wood we have available that is suitable for handles in the first place, and as if that's not enough, there are of course our hands themselves.

Let's assume that we are going to do an "average"-sized carving—such as any of the carvings in this book—in a wood of "average density," something like Honduras mahogany, weighing in at 986 lb/yd³ (550 kg/m³). The majority of the shaping work will be done with a ¾-in (20mm) straight-sided gouge. Let's also consider ourselves to have "average" hand size and strength.

4 I consider myself of average size and strength, and I want to be able to do relief and round carving for furniture and small- to medium-sized ornaments.

Try a mallet weighing 1 lb 3¼ oz to 1 lb 5 oz (550 to 600g), with a center of balance as close to your hand as possible. It will have a head about 4 in (100mm) long and 1⅛ in (30mm) thick and a finger hollow about ⅜ in (10mm) from the head. A mallet is shown in 2-6 with the correct striking posture, as square onto the handle as is reasonable. Glancing blows and possible damage to your carving may result from the poor posture shown in 2-7.

The last mallet option described indicated that a mallet weighing 1 lb 3¼ oz to 1 lb 5 oz (550 to 600g) would be most appropriate for this formula. The ¾-in (20mm) gouge we have chosen is a middle-of-the-road workhorse, and essential for average-sized work.

The first thing we need is a handle wood that will take a reasonable amount of battering on the end of its grain, without splitting. The compression strength of the "end grain" of wood is quite different from that of its long grain, and not all wood is suitable. Two that are well known and often used are European beech and mountain ash. Those that would be unsuitable would be "grainy" softwoods like Douglas fir and Monterey pine.

2-7. A glancing blow to the chisel handle may result in damage to your carving.

A collection of some of the world's most common woodcarving chisel handle shapes is shown in 2-8. Note the different lengths, thicknesses, and the mixture of round- and square-edged handles. Each one is made from wood of about the same density and they weigh between 1.4 and 2 oz (40 and 60g).

So which is the average? Why are some hexagonal and some round? What is the characteristic of the hand that can dictate such an "opposite" in a shape that is supposed to be "average"? The answer, of course, is "nothing." The hexagonal handle was designed not for better grip but so the chisel would be less likely to roll off the workbench. It may also have evolved from early times when the craftsman made his own handles by trimming the corners off a square cross-section offcut salvaged from the workshop floor. However, by virtue of its softness and flexibility, the human hand responds better to a curved shape than a square-edged shape. Try it!

The next thing to look at is the balance of the tool. Remember, in the section preceding this, on mallets, we said that for better control the balance of the mallet should be skewed towards your hand and not its head. It is even more important that the chisel conform to this observation, as it is in your hand all the time, whereas a mallet is a "part-time" tool. You want control directed by your hand, and not by the blade of the chisel, so the weight of the chisel should be more in the hand than top-heavy and in its blade.

Now check your chisel. Chances are that if you check: the balance of your chisel as shown in 2-9, it will be blade heavy. This compares a similar blade with different handles. The blade-heavy handle is European ash of about 1230 lb/yd^3 (700 kg/m^3) and the heavy handle is native Australian gidgee of about 2340 lb/yd^3 (1330 kg/m^3)—an inland desert wattle, used for about 40,000 years by the Australian aborigine for boomerangs and other tools and weapons.

If after trying in your hand a hexagonal handle and a round handle you prefer the round one, it is not surprising. What will be even less surprising is that you will also most likely prefer a handle that is significantly heavier than your current one. This is not to say that the "out-of-balance" one is not good, but that the "handle-heavy" one is better. What you need to decide is whether a better hand feel offering more control, and therefore potential for a better carving result, is more or less important than a less comfortable and less

2-8. Your hand may respond better to a round handle than a square-edged one.

controllable chisel that might not fall on the floor. In other words, you need to establish your comfort zone and make your decision accordingly.

What is all but guaranteed is that a round handle made from a wood like Australian gidgee will feel so superior to the lightweight hexagonal handle that you will want to change all your chisel handles! There was never a better feeling.

2-9. Better control is achieved if the handle of the tool is heavier than the blade, placing the weight of the tool back into the hand.

Using Carving Chisels

Of greatest importance of all is the necessity to ensure the safe handling of the chisels you are using. The kinds of cut you will most likely give yourself are small nicks from touching the sharp end while reaching for a chisel or while sharpening. Surface nicks can bleed more than you would expect, so be careful not to stain the wood you are working on. Blood will soak in to the cells of the wood and it is impossible to get out.

If you are careless enough to hold a piece of wood in one hand and a chisel in the other, and slice the hand holding the wood, you may cause considerable damage requiring stitching or other surgery. It is wise to have a first-aid kit handy in any workshop, and to be familiar with basic first aid, and certainly to know the availability of emergency treatment. Always have your carving stabilized, with both hands free to hold your tools.

A sharp carving chisel will make quite an incision, and the potential for damage must not be underestimated, although if the tools are handled correctly, these sorts of accident are uncommon. Interestingly, children tend to have fewer accidents, and those are also much less severe than adults'—possibly because children are instinctively more careful in unfamiliar situations, and don't take quite so much for granted as adults tend to do.

A slice along the palm of your hand or down the length of your thumb can take some weeks to heal. And if you manage to run a "fluter" (round, deep gouge) upside down along your hand, it will make a double impression and be twice as nasty! Remember that a chisel cut may also introduce other infection from the wood itself or off the bench. We put ourselves at risk from our tendency to rush things and forget that patience is a virtue. Especially in woodcarving! It is not an activity that can be done effectively in a hurry, so do remember to slow down and give yourself a chance. Take it easy, be patient and not too ambitious, take things in a logical order, and you will gain a lot of pleasure from, and learn safe habits in, your woodcarving.

2-10. If your hand is too far from the cutting edge, you may not have the best control over the tool.

Holding the Chisel

Shortly, we'll take a look at a refinement to the gidgee-style handle that will really get you thinking! First, though, we will take a look at how we hold a chisel. A common way of holding a chisel when using a mallet is shown in 2-10. The thumb is pressing against the side of the handle, effectively clamping the chisel between the fingers and thumb. Notice

2-11. Much greater tool control is achieved if you rest the forearm and palm of your hand on the carving.

2-12. *Holding your tool down low restricts your view of it, but once you find your comfort zone, you will have much greater control.*

2-13. *It is important that you find a posture that is relaxed and easy for you. Tension is a distinct disadvantage.*

that the hand is very high on the handle, a long way from the cutting edge. This tends to allow the tool handle to move around a fair bit, and may not be best from a control point of view.

The same action without the mallet is shown in 2-11, the right hand on the handle to both "steer" the chisel and add power to the push. Note that the palm of the left hand (in this case the chisel is being used right-handed) is resting on the work surface, giving total control. The weight of the hands and arms is being fully supported by the cutting edge of the chisel on the wood and the carving itself.

The kind of view you will have when holding the chisel down low is shown in 2-12. You can hardly see the cutting edge at all, and this may initially seem to be a disadvantage. Once again, find your own comfort zone, and this perceived difficulty will disappear. Comfort is extremely important. Experiment until you are comfortable and relaxed, as tension is the last thing you want for satisfactory tool control. An alternative way to hold the gouge is shown in 2-13. This is a very relaxed position, the fingers

of the left hand lightly supporting the shaft held in place by the thumb.

Short, bent tools like the one in 2-14 are awkward to use. If you do not practice a good control grip on these tools, you may find them so hard to handle that you give up on them. They are very useful for creating deeper curves where a straight tool doesn't have the best approach to the wood. Compare 2-15 to 2-14 and you will immediately see the greater and easier control achieved by holding the tool down low.

2-14. *Short, bent tools can be awkward to use if they are not held correctly.*

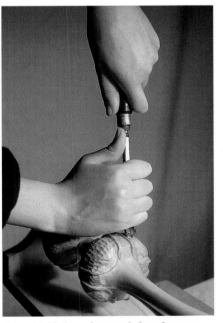

2-15. *Hold short, bent tools low down to make them easier to use.*

Long, bent tools can also be awkward until you get used to them. A long, bent gouge that is 1³⁄₁₆ in (30mm) and almost flat is shown in 2-16 being used to create the flat background in the cartouche from Chapter 12. Because of the shape of the tool shaft, the wrist of the carver's right hand looks quite uncomfortable. To compensate for this necessity, the carver has placed her left hand more comfortably under the blade in 2-17, while at the same time resting it on the carving for greater support. It is a far less tense posture.

The skew chisel, shown in 2-18, requires practice to get completely under control. It is a most versatile tool, and is extremely useful for creating any shape of convex curve. It doubles as a knife, and is great for cleaning up corners. For creating a convex curve, as in 2-18, it is important to be in total control and to be comfortable. Use the tool in a paring motion, pulling it with the fingers of the left hand and steering it with the other. To do this, you will need to "lock" your left wrist, in the case of using it right-handed, onto the surface to stabilize the action. Alternatively, you can push it across the surface, although this may not be as effective, as shown in 2-19. Notice, that you will not have quite the control over the tool if you do this. There is no place to rest your hand or wrist. We have seen, then, that comfort is paramount.

Now let's add a dimension to your handle that will put you completely in charge:

If you hold the chisel firmly in your left hand—the right, if you are left-handed—the mechanics of the hand together with the pressures you are applying tend to push the left thumb up the handle away from the blade. This is reducing the efficiency of the thumb (because it not only tends to slide up the handle but is pushing in the wrong direction), and can even be quite counterproductive depending on how much pressure you are applying. Now, the muscle structure of the thumb, particularly the pad of muscle at the base of it, makes it the strongest finger in your hand. So, let's have it working for us, not against us.

Instead of its pushing up the handle and therefore expending its force in the wrong direction, we will redirect its pressure downwards along the blade and make it work for us. To achieve this, add to your handle a ledge, knob, or knurl that the thumb can push down against, as shown in 2-20.

2-16. Long, bent tools can also be awkward to hold. The left hand wrapped around the shaft increases the likelihood of tension, especially because it is unsupported.

2-17. A much more relaxed posture makes the tool easier to use.

2-18. Use the skew in a paring motion, pulling it with the fingers of the hand resting on the carving; push and steer it with the other.

2-19. Pushing the skew is not always an effective cutting action, because control is limited.

Now you have everything working for you. Your handle has the right shape and balance, you are resting your wrist on the work so that your chisel is only cutting and not also supporting unnecessary weight, and the strongest part of your hand is on the knurl, giving you every bit of control you could ever need. Perfect.

You will not want every handle in your kit to be of this configuration. At the beginning of the discussion we said that one of the design parameters was the task we wanted the chisel to perform. The absolute control that the design in 2-20 affords is best suited to fine

2-20. The knob on the handle allows you to redirect the pressure from the thumb back down the shaft, increasing your control even further.

Avoiding Frustration

For the carver, the most likely recurrent occupational hazard is frustration. This may be a problem that the woodworker who is new to woodcarving especially has to deal with. Annoyance building to the level of frustration will tend to have a very negative effect, not the least of which is to make one quit the craft altogether. To avoid these circumstances, make sure you pace yourself with regard to the degree of difficulty of each new carving you take on, keep sharp tools, and seek advice as to the best wood for your work, or experiment before you launch yourself into a new piece.

Being too ambitious is our most common failing. If you tackle the projects in this book in the order in which they come, you will be doing things in the right order, as they are designed to give you a smooth transition.

Our other greatest failing is that we tend to rush things and forget that patience is a virtue. Especially in woodcarving! It is not an activity that can be done effectively in a hurry, so do remember to slow down and give yourself a chance. Clean surface finishes cannot be achieved with a sharp tool alone. Clean surfaces need time to get there!

Done with all these things in mind, woodcarving is one of the greatest "therapies" you will ever come across. Not only will you feel better, but you will also create attractive and, hopefully, useful things to give to yourself and to others. The finished pieces that you create will give you timeless pleasure from your new craft.

detailing and finishing chisels. It is not the sort of thing that you would want on a 1⅜-in (35mm) gouge for shaping a rocking horse. In fact, for a rocking horse or large sculpture, a lightweight, "blade-heavy" handle is best, because the balance is skewed towards the action end of the tool and not your hand. You get the "punch" where you need it most. So, you will get greatest satisfaction from the knurled handle—fitting it on smaller V-tools, fishtails, and any other favorite finishing chisels you have.

About Knives

A knife or two will be an invaluable addition to your kit. There are many different shapes, some very specifically designed for particular tasks. However, nothing special is needed for any project in this book. You will use a knife for cleaning up your work, getting into places where other tools can't, and it also comes in handy as a scraper for cleaning up some surfaces. As with all other tools, a comfortable grip is needed for best results. A common way of holding a knife for the first time is shown in 2-21. Notice how uncomfortable the index finger looks pushing down hard on the edge of the blade. The manner of holding shown in 2-22 is much more relaxed!

2-21. The index finger bent and pushing hard against the back looks uncomfortable and tense.

2-22. Try relaxing—extend the finger and loosen the grip a little for less tension and better results.

Choosing Chisels

The next step is to consider the chisel itself, and to assess some of the characteristics of these tools so that you might gain a better understanding of how they work and what they are good for. I will be talking in the side boxes about the woodcarving tool itself, the tool shapes, understanding the task of the tool, and the sharpening—grinding, honing, and polishing—of your tools. It is essential that you also read these boxes, as they include commentary on steel thickness that may well affect your choice of tool.

The most important thing to realize about hand tools is that they are very much a personal item. What is comfortable and works for one person may be quite unacceptable for another.

And that is the key: Whatever the case may be, the tool must work for the person using it. The opinions and preferences of another person are, in the end, only of academic interest to the person doing the work. The following discussion tries to keep within this perspective.

"Hard" and "Soft" Steel

Commonly, and most often with good intent, it will be said that the harder the steel, the better, because the tool will hold its "edge" longer and a tool with softer steel is not nearly as "good." In reality, neither case may be correct. It depends a lot on what you want the chisel to actually do. So, let's examine some of the aspects of hard and soft steel:

✽ In woodcarving chisel terms, hard steel may generally mean it is also brittle. Conversely, softer steel may be less brittle. If steel is harder, it will generally also mean that it is harder to sharpen than softer steel and will stay sharper longer (than softer steel).

✽ However, if it is more brittle, it will have a greater tendency to chip or break under pressure, such as when being used in harder wood. This means it may need to be repaired more frequently, and given that it is harder to sharpen than its softer counterpart, it will need a more vigorous maintenance schedule.

✳ Softer steel, on the other hand, will tend to wear rather than break, so it will be theoretically better for harder woods than harder chisels, except that it will require sharpening more often—but most likely without the more vigorous repair schedule.

✳ Logic would have it, then, that a sharp chisel made from harder steel will last a considerable time in softer wood before it needs resharpening, and it will not require much repair work from breakage, chipping, or serration (if used in softer woods).

✳ On the other hand, a chisel fashioned from softer steel may be more ideal for harder woods because it will not tend to break as much, although it will most likely require more frequent sharpening or honing than it would in softer woods.

So, now we have a quandary, don't we? We have to make a decision! Do we go hard steel, or soft steel, or in between? How will we know whether we have hard or soft steel, anyway? Because someone said so? What are we to do?

The answer is quite simple. Make up our own minds, by getting the experiences we need to be able to make our own judgments. And there is only one sure way—and that is to experiment. Try before you buy, call it what you will, but in the end it is your experimentation—and that means experience—that will count. Does this mean that you should buy one of each brand to see what it can do? Probably yes. At least you should borrow chisels from as many people as possible to find out whatever you can. But the best way is to own your own, so you can do whatever you wish with them, to find out just where your comfort zone lies.

Somewhere for you is an acceptable balance between hard and soft steel and hard and soft wood. It may be that your choice will vary over time with the changes in your experience, and it surely will be inevitable that this is so. For you to decide, then, on what is right or wrong or best and worst before you have had your share of experiences would be to prematurely choose between the right combination for tomorrow's job or the wrong thing for today's.

The net of it all, then, is that you must continue to try everything you can, in every form and combination you can, until you start to find your own answers.

The Woodcarving Tool

The woodcarving tool is typically made from steel, to a specification peculiar to each manufacturer. The steel might be hard, soft, brittle, shiny, dull, handmade, machine made, or any combination of these. No two brands will be the same, each having its own characteristics. It is important that over time you get to know your tools. You will want to be familiar with what makes them wear, break, chip, serrate, or become just plain blunt. Obviously usage will do all of these things, but the important thing is what kind of usage?

For example, a handmade carving tool from Thailand will most likely be of soft steel, and will not remain sharp for very long, but will be capable of being very quickly sharpened to an amazing edge. The blades will likely be of comparatively thin steel, which means that you can easily grind the bevel into a long, thin cross section perfect for fine relief carving—which is of course what the Thais do very well. The handle will probably be uncomfortable for most of us, often being no more than a broken piece of branch from a tree.

On the other hand, the typical European and North American tool is made from a modern alloy steel, is significantly harder and sometimes more brittle, and is thicker in cross section. Being more robust than the Thai version, it is good for sculpture in hard wood, provided it is shaped correctly. It will take longer to sharpen than the Thai chisel, but it will also stay sharper longer. Without significant lengthening of the bevel, the blade will probably always be less suitable for very fine relief work. This is not to say it can't be done, just that it is less suitable.

Neither tool is necessarily superior to the other, given the quality of output that is sustainable in Europe by Europeans, North America by North Americans, and in Thailand by Thais. What the Europeans, Americans, and Thais all have in common is that they have adapted to the idiosyncrasies of the tools they have. They adjust themselves and their designs to suit the circumstances of their wood and tools, so that the four elements remain in equilibrium. And this is what you must do, too.

Basic Tool Bevel Shapes

Before we move to the actual sharpening process, we need to take a look at the basic shapes of bevel and what they will each do.

There are three primary shapes of bevel for woodworking tools, each of which relates to the disciplines of carpentry, turning, and carving. These three primary shapes form the platform of all tool shaping and sharpening principles for these disciplines. We will see that the angle of the bevel dictates the behavior of the tool.

TYPE 1, THE FLAT BEVEL A carpenter is essentially concerned with cutting through wood in straight lines such as to make a mortise or a tenon, so the carpenter's chisel has a flat back, a flat face, a flat bevel, and flat sides. There are variations on the theme, but essentially that is what it is. For creating a flat edge, the turner and carver will also generally use a flat tool.

TYPE 2, THE CONVEX BEVEL A convex bevel, on the other hand, will push the tool away from the surface of the wood. If the tool has dug into the surface, the tendency of the bevel will be to push the tool up and out. The greater the convexity, the greater this tendency. Further, a less convex bevel will lower the angle of approach of the tool to the wood surface, and a greater curvature will increase the angle of approach. More on this later.

Because a carpenter wants to cut flat, it is unlikely his/her tool will have a convex bevel. A wood turner would have a convex bevel for creating a concave curve, such as the inside of a bowl. So would a woodcarver have a convex bevel for creating concave shapes.

TYPE 3, THE CONCAVE BEVEL A concave bevel will create a set of conditions the opposite of the convex bevel—the tool will have a tendency to nosedive into the wood. The greater the concavity, the greater this tendency. A carpenter will most likely never have a concave bevel, because it won't help achieve the objective of cutting flat. A wood turner will have a concave bevel—it is also called "hollow ground"—to help create convex curves on a spindle. A woodcarver might have a concave bevel on a skew to assist in the creation of convex shapes like beads.

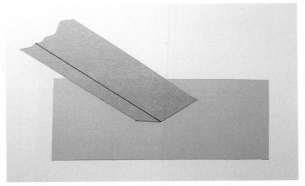

TYPE 1, THE FLAT BEVEL. When it is against the wood surface, it will move along flat (provided it is of course held consistently at the angle of the bevel). This tool will cut a flat shape.

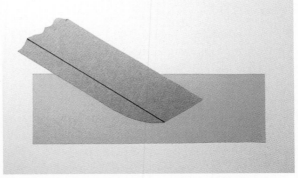

TYPE 2, THE CONVEX BEVEL. When it is against the wood's surface, it will push the tool out of the wood, and this will result in cutting a concave shape.

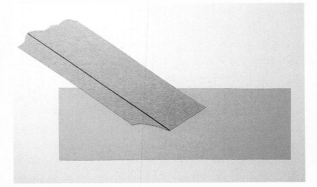

TYPE 3, THE CONCAVE BEVEL. When it is against the wood surface, it will push the tool into the wood, and this will result in cutting a convex shape. It may also mean the tool nosedives into the surface.

Secondhand Chisels

For many of us, price is a major consideration, and very often we will find ourselves looking at second-hand tools as a possible way of saving money or adding to our collection tools that are no longer available from modern manufacturers. Are old tools worth buying?

There is no easy answer to this question, unless you are a collector of tools and actually using them is of a secondary, if any, consideration. If usage is more important, there are some things that should be kept in mind:

For all intents and purposes it is impossible to know the history of the tool and therefore to know whether or not it has been mistreated, particularly in the sharpening process. If this is the case, and the tool has been over-heated, chances are that the steel consistency has been altered, making it too soft to hold an edge for any reasonable length of time. It may be that the steel has become quite "crumbly" and hardly usable at all. Sometimes you can tell this by the color of the metal—if it is blue, then certainly be aware that it may not be a usable instrument. The tool has surely "lost its temper."

With many "vintage" tools the manufacturing procedure was to temper (basically this means to harden the steel by a heat-treatment process) the blade for a short distance, say, 1 to 1³⁄₁₆ in (25 to 30mm) from the sharp end. If the chisel is well worn down through usage, then this tempered part will mostly be gone, making the tool of limited if any use for further work. Therefore avoid tools that are worn out.

One of the greatest enemies of the tool owner is rust, which I discuss in the accompanying side boxes on sharpening. Any tool pitted from rust along or near the cutting edge is most likely a poor proposition. Rust may also hide chipped or cracked steel. Careful examination of the tool should reveal whether or not there are any fine cracks in the blade, resulting either from misuse or general deterioration.

The age of the tool itself may well render it unusable. Depending on the formula of the steel and its treatment over the years, the blade may simply be suffering from old age. The metal may have recrystallized, for example, and become too brittle to be of use.

All in all, the older the chisel most likely the less attractive it is as a working tool. The younger the tool, the better.

The Woodcarver's Special Needs

A woodcarver is concerned with the creation of shadows by the development of irregular (meaning not geometric) compound (multiple) convex and concave curves that interrelate (are joined together) and are interdependent (rely on one another for the design effect).

To do this, the woodcarver needs tools that are capable of creating any shape whatsoever, and therefore there can be no certainty as to their shape. The tools that are good for one project may not be good enough for another. This does not mean that new tools need to be purchased all the time, but it may mean that some tools need to be "sharpened" (meaning ground) in a different way to make them effective for a particular purpose.

What we mean by "no certainty" is that it is unreasonable to say that a particular tool must always be the same shape and you must only ever grind it a certain way. Here are several statements typical of what is said about sharpening—each of which is the kind of "rule" that should be actively discouraged: "It must be flat across the face" (the face is the cutting edge); "A gouge must not have shoulders that point backwards or forwards" (the shoulder is the corner of the cutting face); "The bevel must be 27 degrees"; "The bevel must be flat"; "The bevel must be concave."

The truth is, the tool shape can be anything, provided it works successfully in your hands for the purpose for which it is intended.

And if it is to work for the purpose for which it is intended, it must be in equilibrium not only with the wood to be carved, but with the design requirements of the carving and you, who are to do the carving. What works for one person may not work for another. Therefore, we need to understand the task that we expect the chisel to do, and shape it accordingly, in a manner suitable for the user. So before we can even start carving, we need to achieve an understanding of the task that we expect the chisel to perform. And that is what tool sharpening is all about: nothing more, nothing less, than an understanding.

Understanding the Task of the Tool

We carvers need to develop a management technique that enables us to get the best out of our tools. And this may involve grinding a tool bevel to precisely 27 degrees, although it is unlikely that the average person would actually ever be able to do this. However, it will more likely involve experimentation for each individual carver, so that each person will develop his or her own sharpening techniques that best suit their personal characteristics and the designs and wood they are carving.

The woodcarver is generally concerned with scooping material out. The chisel that the carver uses has a bevel such that when you push the chisel into the wood it comes back out again. For that reason, the bevel on the carver's chisel is generally convex. If it were concave like the turner's chisel, when you went to push it through the wood it would not come out—it would nose-dive into it. It would get stuck. Literally. The important thing to remember, then, is that the woodcarver grinds the bevel on his chisel the opposite way the turner does for convex cutting and the same way the turner does for concave cutting. For the carver, flat is good, slightly convex is better, and concave is rare.

By the same token, the carver needs to pay attention to the amount of convexity that is ground into bevels. If it is too much, the angle of approach of the tool into the wood is too high, and this makes the chisel too hard to use. Too much energy is needed to force the chisel into the wood and through it at the same time.

Sometimes it may be a good idea to have a high approach into the wood, such as for deep cutting of a concave curve like the side of a bowl. On the other hand it may be better to use an appropriate tool shaped for the purpose—such as a long or short bent gouge, which by virtue of the shape of the shaft has a higher approach to the surface.

To enable us to begin to decide the most appropriate design for our cutting edge, we need to understand what each of the three primary bevel shapes (described in the box on page 26) will do for our carving tools.

Which Shape to Buy?

There is an amazing variety of carving tool shapes, so much so that to the beginner the choices are seemingly so great as to be too daunting. In reality, however, the confusion can be cleared up if we take a look at the logic of the variations that are available for carving tools. Of greatest importance is for us to realize right away that, in terms of the average, only a few tools are really needed—at most, between one and two dozen. The many others available may be thought of as being there for special purposes that occur from time to time but not very often.

Historically, there are varying names for the same tool, and varying manufacturer's numbering systems of shapes and sizes. The tools are normally given a number to allow them to be identified. Unfortunately these numbering systems also vary among countries as well as manufacturers. None of this makes it any easier for the novice who is eager to start off with the right set of tools. There is no great point in my presenting history in these pages, as there are sufficient books available with adequate coverage of the subject. However, I will take a look at the basics of shape and size that are commonly available in today's context:

In simplest terms, there are really only four categories of tools: the chisel, the gouge, parting tools, and knives.

2-23. These almost flat gauges are all that are necessary of this style for the projects in this book. The sizes are measured in a straight line from shoulder to shoulder, and are ¾ in (20mm), ½ in (12mm), ¼ in (6mm), and ⅛ in (3mm), moving from left to right.

2-24. *You will also need a ¾-in (20mm) skew, a 1⅛-in (30mm) almost flat, long bent gouge, an 8mm V-tool, and a knife.*

The Straight Chisel

The straight chisel is flat across the face, and is sometimes referred to as a "firmer" chisel. It is like a carpenter's chisel, but has a bevel on both sides. It is used for trimming edges flat, and is particularly useful for borders, for example. You will not use one very often, and none is necessary for the projects in this book. A carpenter's chisel will generally do in its place, if you feel you need one. You will most likely be better off with almost flat gouges, like those in 2-23, because the

2-25. *These rounder deep gouges, also sometimes called "fluters," are all that are necessary for the projects in this book. The sizes are, from left to right, ½ in (12mm), ½ in (12mm, but shallower), ¼ in (6mm), and ⅛ in (3mm).*

corners will not dig in and leave tracks that need to be cleaned off. The almost flat gouge has very slightly raised corners (shoulders), which clear the surface without digging in.

One straight chisel you will use constantly is the "skew," like the one in 2-24. It is the most versatile of all carving tools, and once you master it you will never be without it. It could probably be referred to as a specialty shape, but it is so useful and common that it is included as a "straight" chisel.

The Gouge

The more deeply curved varieties, such as those shown in 2-25, are also sometimes referred to by their older name, "fluters." The ¾-in (20mm) gouge of the flatter shape as in 2-23 is the workhorse tool of the carver. It is robust and can take constant hitting with a mallet, has a straight shaft as opposed to the tapered shaft of varieties also known as "fishtails." It is important when buying your workhorse tools to ensure that they are strong enough to take continuous mallet work. It is not appropriate to use fine-shafted tools such as fishtails with a mallet.

Bevel Shape and Carving

In order to decide on the best design for our cutting edge, we need to understand what each of the three primary bevel shapes will do for our carving tools. The three basic bevel shapes are shown here in relation to the skew, the simplest (and at the same time the most useful and diversified) of the entire carver's tools. The decision as to the right curve will depend on what you want the tool to do.

FLAT-BEVEL SKEW. The best way to think about flat bevels is to think of them as being neutral. They will not encourage the tool to dig in or push out. The tool in this will only go where you put it, without favoring any direction, and with no ability to do anything other than cut straight ahead. You will only be able to grind it flat on the flat of the wheel (i.e., the side of the wheel), so don't put it on the edge of the wheel (the circumference). When you use your slipstone, which we will discuss shortly, you must also hold it flat to the surface of the stone.

CONCAVE-BEVEL SKEW. The bevel is ground hollow, or concave, by using the edge of the grinding wheel. The concave bevel has a tendency to nosedive the tool into the wood. For cutting a convex curve like this one, logic would suggest that this bevel shape is better than the flat one. And, indeed, it is. A slight concavity in the bevel will also enable you to create a longer, thinner bevel towards the cutting edge, and this will allow you to make a finer cutting edge that will be sharper. Because the steel will be thinner, it will also be weaker, and this may not be appropriate for harder woods.

CONVEX-BEVEL SKEW. This would be created using the flat face of the grinding wheel. As we said, this shape would tend to push the tool upwards, so for creating the convex curve shown here, this shape would only make the tool more difficult to handle. It will want to slide off the surface all the time. If you try this with your skew, you will in fact find that it almost feels slippery in this configuration on a convex surface. It can be hard to control and hard to get it to cut. Part of the problem is the high angle of the approach of the tool to the wood, and part is the thicker steel at the cutting edge, making the tool not quite as sharp.

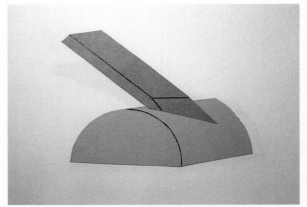

FLAT-BEVEL SKEW. A flat bevel is "neutral" and will not encourage the tool to dig in or push out.

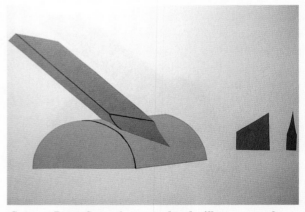

CONCAVE-BEVEL SKEW. A concave bevel will encourage the skew, in this example, to follow the contour of the convex surface and make it easier to use.

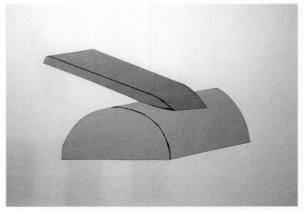

CONVEX-BEVEL SKEW. A convex bevel in this situation will make the tool harder to use.

2-26. This is the profile of a short bent gouge.

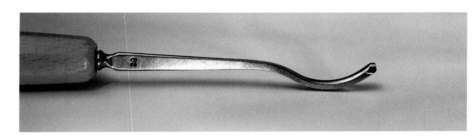

2-27. This is the profile of a long bent gouge.

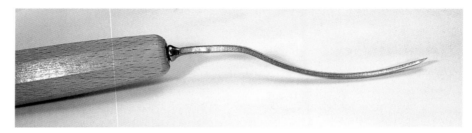

2-28. This is the profile of a reverse bent gouge.

Gouges also come with different curves to the shaft, such as short bent, long bent, and reverse bent (sometimes called "back bent"). The short bent is useful for creating concave surfaces such as bowls, the long bent for getting into difficult-to-access areas that aren't as deep as bowls, and the reverse bent for undercutting edges. Its bevel is on the reverse side of the tool, so it works in reverse for cutting in behind rather than off the top (see 2-26, 2-27, and 2-28).

Parting Tools

The V-tool, or parting tool, is generally available in different angles, normally 90, 60, and 45 degrees (refer to 2-24). Sometimes it is available with a rounded apex rather than a true "V," as is the case in 2-24. The V-tool is primarily used for marking out patterns—particularly in relief carving. It is also used to some extent for general decoration. It can be used for such applications as lettering, creating vertical edges, and crosshatching. It also comes in short bent and long bent varieties.

Specialty Shapes

There are many specialty shapes, only a few of which are necessary for the projects in this book. See 2-29. You will also see such names as "fluteroni," "backeroni," and "macaroni" in different catalogues.

2-29. There are many specialty shapes shown in manufacturers' catalogues, but the only ones needed for the projects are, from left to right, a ⅜ in (10mm) reverse bent, a ⅜-in (10mm) short bent, a ¾-in (20mm) long bent, a ⅝-in (15mm) long bent, and a 4mm long bent.

The Shape of the Cutting Edge

Once you have decided which bevel curve is most appropriate, it will be necessary to consider the most appropriate shape for the face or end (cutting edge) of the tool. The face, once again, can be flat, concave, convex, or any other shape, depending on what you want the tool to do.

FLAT-FACE TOOL. This edge will make a square flat incision in the wood. This is appropriate if you always want a square cut—because it can't do anything else. It is convenient, but not essential, for getting clearing cuts to meet stop-cuts (see Chapter 5, "You Can Start Carving Now!"). It is inconvenient if you are carving in a concave curve, because the shoulders will want to dig into the curved surface. It is also inconvenient if you want to do a lot of scroll work in which you want to roll or twist (like a corkscrew) the chisel—the shoulders will want to dig in then, too.

CONVEX-FACE TOOL. With the convex-face tool, you have the greatest versatility of movement; however, you might also need a bit more practice to get a uniform depth of cut if you use a tool with this sort of face for stop-cuts. Clearly the center of the gouge would dig in further than the remainder, requiring you to roll the tool slightly to even out the depth of the cut. For a tool that you use mainly for clearing large amounts of waste, you might have a relatively flat face, and for the tools that are used for shaping, a convex or raked-back shoulder may be an advantage. Certainly if there is to be scroll work done, this style is very convenient. You can roll the tool very easily without the shoulders' getting in the way.

HOLLOW-FACE TOOL. This is not really a convenient shape for much at all, because the shoulders will always dig in first. This will make it difficult for clearing waste in pretty much every situation except where you are making a lot of "beads" (see Chapter 7 "Over and Over"). If the concave curve matches the diameter of the beads, then it may be useful for quickly clearing waste from around the base of each bead. You would need an additional tool to make the stop-cut, since the shoulders would dig in further than the middle and make an incision of uneven depth.

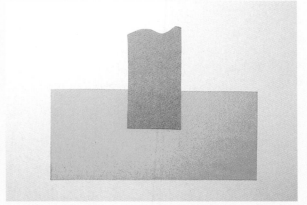

FLAT-FACE TOOL. A flat face is convenient for getting clearing cuts to meet stop-cuts, but inconvenient for scroll work.

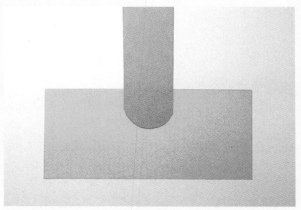

CONVEX-FACE TOOL. A convex face is very useful for scroll work. There are no shoulders to get in the way.

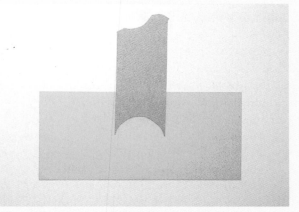

HOLLOW-FACE TOOL. A hollow face is not much use for anything because the shoulders will always dig in first.

Benches and Other Holding Devices

In the majority of situations, unless using a mallet, the carver will hold the carving tool in both hands. Not only is this most sensible from the practical point of view, but it is also safest. It is imperative, then, that the carver give careful consideration to the stability of the wood during the carving process.

First, comfort. Whether to sit or stand will depend a lot on the ease of doing one or the other during a particular carving process. However, if standing, the hardness of the floor surface and the bench height are very important, to help avoid aching legs and back. A thick rubber mat to stand on is very useful, or a wooden floor instead of a concrete one. Something with "give" is much better than a solid base.

For most people, the top of the bench (the work surface), for standing, should be at the same height as the forearm when it is bent at the elbow with the upper arm perpendicular and forearm horizontal to the ground. Also for most people, if the height is as little as 2 in (50mm) too low or too high, then backache will result.

The traditional workbench has long been the "normal" facility for holding the wood being carved, whether the wood is clamped to the surface or held in a vise of some kind. However, there is one significant limitation to the traditional bench. Unless the carver is ambidextrous, able to swap between being left-handed and right-handed at will, then each time it is necessary to change carving direction, the work will have to be turned around. Either that or the carver will have to walk around the bench and reach the work from the other side. This normally would not be practical, unless the bench were in the middle of the floor and not against the wall.

So the carver will have to ensure that whatever he or she decides is consistent with whatever degree of skill he or she has or is prepared to achieve. In the long run, it is better to train to be ambidextrous, as this will save a considerable amount of trouble.

The best combination of all, however, is to be able to walk around the bench—and be ambidextrous as well. To this end, the carver can develop the skill required for this dexterity, and the best work surface is a smallish size, say, a two-foot-square (600 by 600mm) work surface for most common applications. The bench can be located in the middle of the floor space, giving free access from all sides.

Hazards from Wood and Wood Dust

Woodcarving can be done not only with hand chisels, but also with rasps, files, saws, electric chisels, rotary burs and knives, sanding discs, and chain saws. Each of these tools also creates wood dust of varying particle sizes, and this wood dust can be a major hazard.

Wood dust can cause a variety of problems, such as serious skin allergies and skin irritation, eye inflammation, respiratory diseases such as hay fever and asthma, pneumonia and lung fibrosis, and nasal carcinoma. The wood itself may contain sap and the surface of the wood may be covered with fungus and other plant matter that may also be dangerous. This is particularly so if the wood is freshly cut (i.e., is "green"). Fungus growing on the outside of a tree trunk is shown below. Particles from fungi like this can be easily breathed in or enter your system through a cut in your finger. Wear a dust mask, gloves, and eye protection if you are cutting wood. It is easy for fungus to grow in the warm and moist internal environment of your lungs. Major life-threatening disease can result.

Wear glasses, a dust mask, and eye protection to help prevent life-threatening illness from fungus.

Grinding, Honing, and Polishing Tools

By "grinding, honing, and polishing tools," we mean the personal process by which you manage your tools—commonly known as "sharpening." Something that does not make sense within the context of woodcarving is the setting up of a "book of rules" about sharpening. The establishment of a set of principles, yes, but of rules, no. This is because the chisel should be managed by you to achieve the results you want from the piece of wood you are using. This management process requires the application of various sharpening principles to the circumstances that arise from the coming together of your wood, the chosen design, and not the least, yourself.

Managing Your Tools

You must do everything you can to develop the ability to manage your tools so that they work in such a way as to produce the results you want. To achieve this, you need to arrange an equilibrium between those four elements:

> THE TOOL,
> THE WOOD,
> THE DESIGN,
> AND YOU.

If you stick to a set of hard and fast rules about sharpening, then you are making the process of equilibrium that much more difficult, because you are making a "given" out of one or more of the variables in the equation. What I will discuss in these boxes regarding the process of sharpening is a set of principles for each of the four factors, so that we can make the process of equilibrium swift and sure.

Principles of Sharpening

Let us begin, then, and put together our shopping list of sharpening principles.

To get started, here are some fundamental observations that you can try for yourself. All you need is some hard and some soft wood, and a gouge. You could put together your own set of experiences like the following:

✳ A hard and dense wood requires significantly more energy to push a chisel through than a softer and less dense wood; therefore a mallet will most likely be used.

✳ A thin blade is easier to push through wood than a thicker blade; therefore bevels that are longer will be easier to use than bevels that are shorter (see also the boxes on page 30 and 32).

✳ A thin blade will chip, serrate, or break more easily than a thick one, especially in denser woods; therefore a shorter bevel (which makes the cutting edge thicker) may be more appropriate (see also the boxes on page 30 and 32).

✳ If the chisel is not shaped correctly for the wood, a softer wood is more likely to tear than a firmer wood, which is more likely to break or fracture. Therefore, if either of these occurs, the tool bevel shape needs reassessment.

✳ A softer wood is more likely to be spongy and squash when compressed, particularly through the end grain. A harder wood will generally cut more cleanly through the end grain, but the harder it gets the more likely it is to fracture than cut. Therefore, the thinner blade is the better for this application (see the second point above).

✳ A wood with a comparatively large "cell" in its cellular makeup—especially one with thin or weak "walls" (like balsa wood)—will crumble under pressure from a thick chisel. If this occurs, then a thinner blade may be better.

✳ Soft steel will wear more quickly than harder steel, particularly where the resistance of the wood is greater, such as with denser species. Harder steel will chip more easily in denser wood. Since chipping is more difficult to repair than wearing, harder steel may not be appropriate for harder woods.

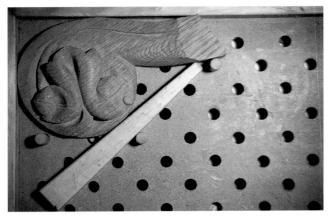

2-30. *A pegboard with wedges is a quick and easy holding device.*

Pegboards, Cam Tops, and Newspaper

For most carving, you will need to be able to easily remove the workpiece from the workbench. A simple pegboard is shown in 2-30 that can be clamped to the bench with a C-clamp. Wedges between the carving and the movable pegs hold the carving secure.

The pegs are replaced with eccentric cams shown in 2-31 that have a dowel pivot that sits in a hole in the baseboard. Make sure the position of the pivot is off center so that the perimeter of the round head of the cam locks against the carving.

A combination of pegs is seen in 2-32, locked up close to the carving, plus newsprint glued with water-soluble glue between the carving and the base. Slip a spatula into the paper and it will give way, and any left on can be removed with water. Cereal box cardboard is very useful for this technique.

2-31. *Eccentric cams make a convenient and very effective holding system.*

2-32. *Newspaper or light cardboard can be glued (with water-soluble glue) between the carving and the base. Pry off the carving when finished.*

The Process of Shaping, Sharpening, and Polishing

The process of chisel preparation and performance maintenance revolves around the three activities of grinding, honing with the slipstone, and polishing with a strop:

1 GRINDING

Grinding establishes the basic shape of the cutting edge. Grinding the tool on a grinding wheel is the kind of thing you would do only if you chip or break the chisel, or if it wears out of shape, or if you want to reshape it to make it more appropriate for the work you are trying to do (see A through F).

It is important to watch for normal wear on the bevel. The chisel will wear most often at the end of the bevel near the cutting edge; obviously that is where all the work is done! And in effect a secondary bevel is created about 1/16 inch (one or two millimeters) back from the cutting edge (refer to E). If you continue to sharpen the tool without removing this secondary bevel, you'll find the tool will become harder and harder to use; you will think it is still blunt and keep sharpening it the same way, and make things worse and worse. The developing secondary bevel needs to be ground off with the grinding wheel or slipstone. The secondary bevel increases the angle of approach of the chisel to the wood, increasing the resistance of the wood to the cutting action.

Achieving a Convex Bevel

The way that the woodcarver achieves a convex bevel, as opposed to a concave, is by using the face (side) of the wheel. Because there is a flat surface on the side of the wheel as opposed to the edge (circumference), you can grind the chisel into any curve you want. Never let a woodturner sharpen your carving gouge unless he knows this, as he will invariably hollow-grind it because he will automatically place the bevel onto the circumference of the wheel and transfer that curve into the bevel of your chisel.

The grade of abrasive the wheel is made from is also extremely important. Too coarse and too much

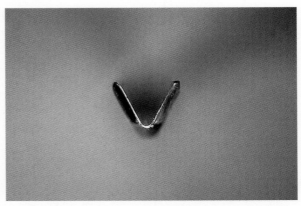

A. The chip is visible as a small black dot on the left of this V-tool. This chip will make a raised ridge on the surface of your wood and it will look as though it is scratched.

B. Not only is this V-tool broken, but it has no clearly defined bevel, and rust is starting to form on the surface.

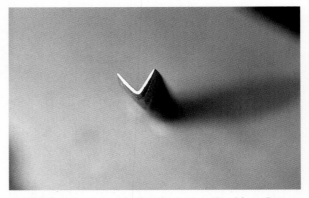

C. The first step in regrinding the broken V-tool is to flatten the cutting edges, at the same time making them at right angles to the shaft, which is the most convenient shape for most carving situations.

D. Overheating on a grinding wheel will cause burning of the steel. Regularly dip the tool in cold water and don't apply undue pressure.

E. Rust is also starting to form on this gouge. The secondary bevel is also clearly visible about a third of the way between the cutting edge and the original heel, which is the place where the bevel begins.

F. The reground gouge has a clear, even, continuous bevel and is ready for touching up on a slipstone before polishing on a strop.

damage will be done. For carving tools, grit of around 120, closely compacted to make a smooth surface, is ideal, not coarsely packed because this makes the surface too rough. A speed of around 1,400 rpm is quite acceptable. Be sure a tin of water is available to keep the tool from overheating. Generally the finer the abrasive and the faster the wheel, the greater the likelihood the tool will get too hot and burn (see D). Water wheels are useful sometimes but can be a bit slow, although they do offer good control. Most water wheels allow grinding only on their circumference (edge). A horizontal grinder is best because it allows easy access to the flat expanse of the side of the wheel.

A variety of tool-holding jigs and rests are available to guide you in the grinding process. Use them by all means, although avoid them if you can, simply because if you master freehand grinding, you will find that it is generally more accurate and is faster. You also develop and maintain the "feel" for what you are doing, which in the end gives you greater control, and therefore greater speed and accuracy.

Ideally, you will grind the tool so that there are no facets on it from the wheel. To do this, it is best to stand in a comfortable position with a good balance and freedom to move without restriction. Loosen up and relax. If you are rigid and tense, you will not be able to grind the tool with a smooth action, and you will surely end up with the bevel covered in facets. If the grinding wheel spins towards you, you will have greater opportunity for control of the tool; most wheels are electrically wired or mechanically geared this way. If you are rigging up your own wheel, and you have it spinning away from you, be sure to at least test both ways. If the wheel spins away from you, you will probably find that the tool will tend to pull away from you, and this dragging effect will reduce the control you have over it. Moving towards you is significantly better. Try it!

At the end of the shaping process, the tool will likely be covered in scratches from the revolving stone. These scratches must be removed so that the cutting edge is as fine and smooth as possible—actually polished. Then the tool is really sharp. The gouge in F has been ground on a fine wheel. It will not need much work on a slipstone.

The Process of Shaping, Sharpening, and Polishing

2 HONING WITH THE SLIPSTONE

A slipstone is used for the part of the process called honing, a term derived from the Old English Anglo Saxon word *han*, meaning "stone." Honing prepares the cutting edge for polishing.

Not a Flat Bench Stone

A small slipstone such as the one shown in G is generally much better to use than a regular flat bench stone. The bench stone is designed for sharpening carpenters' chisels and plane irons and the like—cutting tools that have flat bevels. The carving chisel's bevel is not necessarily flat, plus there is the lateral curve of the tool in the first place, so you need to be able to see what you're doing. If you are holding the tool down on the bench, then you're hardly able to see it (the bevel) at all. So we use a little slipstone by rocking the chisel on its curve and rolling the stone over the complete surface of the bevel. You are in effect rolling the stone around the chisel, *not* the chisel around the stone. The reason for this is that you have greater control if you move the stone and not the tool. Try it!

How to Hold the Stone

You must hold the chisel and slipstone in such a position that you can easily see everything you are doing, generally between the thumb and the index finger. It is important to "work" the entire surface of the bevel, otherwise you will have a greater likelihood of ending up with a secondary style of bevel near the cutting edge by working the stone too much near the cutting edge and not enough over the whole area. Avoid holding the stone at an angle like that in H.

What Shape and Size of Stone?

There are a great variety of shapes and sizes and different materials for slipstones; however, if in doubt, stick to the traditional fine, hard, "original" Arkansas stones—they are excellent.

G. Hold a small slipstone so you can see exactly what you are doing. Move the stone around the tool for best control and therefore greater accuracy.

H. Work the slipstone evenly over the entire bevel area, avoiding creating secondary bevels or rounding off the cutting edge, which is what will happen if you hold the stone at an angle like this.

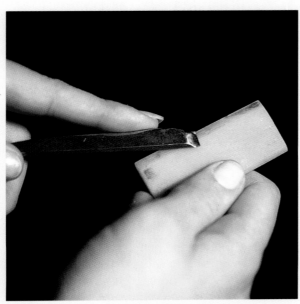

I. Removing a burr from the inside of a V-tool like this will dig a hole in the apex of the "V" and the tool will need regrinding. The apex of the "V" is generally rounded and is not a perfect point at all. If you grind the outside to a perfect point, and the inside is round, you will create a blunt spot at the apex. You must grind the outside to the same shape as the inside so the two surfaces come together to form the sharp edge that you need.

J. Be sure to hold the slipstone flat along the shaft.

Which Lubricant?

Some people spit on it (the slipstone). Some use kerosene, water, mineral oil, cooking oil, and a hundred other things no doubt! It is suggested you try neat's-foot oil. It is essentially boiled-down offal. The leftovers, originally made for use as a leather preservative, are still used for that purpose. "Neat" is another Old English word derived from Anglo-Saxon times—*neat,* meaning "cow" or "ox."

It has some advantages over mineral oil:

1. First, it doesn't clog the stone in quite the same way. It still will, but it is easier to remove, and not quite so gluggy. Wash your stones regularly with hot water and detergent (laundry soap is OK). Scrub them with a fingernail brush. A clogged stone cannot cut the steel of the chisel, so it is quite useless.

2. Neat's-foot oil is a skin softener, so if you are unwilling to cover your fingers with irritating mineral oil, then try nature's own!

3. The surface tension is different from mineral oil, so when you are grinding on the slipstone, the fine steel particles that are ground off are floated away from the cutting edge. They do not congregate around it, as with mineral oil, so you are less likely to be grinding steel on steel—which will inhibit the "cutting" action of the stone.

4. And finally, it is traditional, for whatever worth you place on that. Chances are, it was all that was available to the early woodworker, mineral oil and petroleum derivatives not being in plentiful supply at the time!

As you grind with your slipstone, you will eventually get a fine burr forming on the side opposite to which you are grinding with the stone. You can feel it with your finger on the inside of the chisel if you are grinding the bevel. Once you get that burr, it's a signal to stop grinding with the slipstone on the outside of the bevel and start on the inside—to remove it. It will possibly "roll" from side to side until it breaks off. If you push it through a piece of softwood, is should come off immediately. It is important not to damage the tool while you are removing the burr (see I and J).

The Process of Shaping, Sharpening, and Polishing

3 POLISHING WITH A STROP

Once you've ground the chisel with the slipstone, you will notice the little scratches that you've made on the bevel. If you look at them under a magnifying glass, you'll see the surface is badly scratched (it might be circles or straight lines from the slipstone or left over from the grinding wheel), so you don't have a smooth surface but in fact a rough one. There will in fact be a rough surface on both top and bottom (bottom = bevel side) of the chisel. On both sides of the chisel's cutting edge there is a rough surface, so where these rough surfaces meet at the cutting edge there is a doubly rough edge. To create a fine-cutting blade, these scratches must be removed. The only way to get rid of them is to polish them off.

The Strop

Polishing can be done with a strop. The most common strop is simply quality leather. Cow belly hide is perfect. You could add some additional abrasive for faster cutting, such as 1,000-grain silicon carbide or aluminum oxide. Occasional application of neat's-foot oil will preserve the leather and help adhere the abrasive powder to the surface. You could have two strops, one with and one without the additional abrasive.

The way to use the strop is to draw the chisel right down the full length of the strop, rolling the chisel on its curve at the same time. Apply a bit of pressure, and get a bit of speed up, and you'll very quickly achieve a polished surface. Provided you had a burr in the beginning, which means that both surfaces in fact met one another, you will then have a sharp chisel (see K).

Reflected Light

If you hold your chisel so that the light hits the sharp edge, and you can see a shiny white line along the sharp edge, then it is in fact not sharp enough. With the naked eye, you should not be able to see any reflected light along a sharp edge.

The final test for sharpness is of course that the chisel cuts the wood cleanly and easily.

By setting up your own standard test you will always get the same result. For example, jelutong, which is an unforgiving wood if you try to cut it with a blunt chisel, will soon tell you whether or not you have a sharp edge. You will hear it tear the fibers if it is blunt and slice through them when it is sharp; you will see the torn surface fibers if it is blunt and see the crisp surface when it is sharp, and you will also be able to feel the difference.

K. To polish the tool, draw the bevel down a strop. You could make different-shaped strops for polishing the topside of your tools—leather around a dowel for deep "fluters" (round, deep gouges), for example.

Lighting as a Tool

Lighting is not normally regarded as a "tool"; however, it is of such importance that I consider it essential to include it in the lineup.

We saw in Chapter 1 how the impact of lighting can have a major influence on the shadows that we see, and hence the work that we achieve. There is no substitute for having the most correct lighting for the particular situation. So, let's take a look at some of the more common situations and see just what is the most appropriate lighting to choose.

For relief carving, the light by which you work will be critical. The finer the detail, the more critical it will be, as the detail of the work will be clearly seen only in light that forms good shadows.

At the other end of the spectrum, a large, chunky sculpture for the garden will require a far less specific lighting setup, and probably the ambient light in the garden will be perfect.

If, for example, you are able to carve only by naturally available light, then the best shadow-forming light is during the morning and the afternoon when the sun is low and the shadows are long. This light is best during autumn, winter, and spring, when the sun is generally low relative to the horizon.

In the northern hemisphere the least shadow-forming light will be the ambient light from the north, and in the southern hemisphere the south. Therefore, for natural light, the best time to carve in relief will be morning or afternoon during winter with the light coming from the south for the northern hemisphere and from the north for the southern hemisphere.

Unfortunately, of course, the light will never be constant, either in intensity, depending on clouds or position, because of relative movement of earth and sun, and this will be a source of frustration. Try it, though, and you will soon see it is the "ultimate" in lighting for shadow.

Transferring Patterns with Carbon Paper

Not always available in these "modern" times, carbon paper is a relic from the days of typing pools and typewriters. It is very useful, however, for transferring patterns from original material. Care will need to be taken that the carbon isn't too worn out, that the stylus used leaves a clear line neither too thick nor blurred, and that the pattern is held in one place for

---

Safety and Lighting

In addition to allowing you to see what you are doing, lighting is important in preventing potential headaches and damage to your eyes. If you find you are getting frequent headaches from your workshop activity, make sure you check the lighting that you use as well as check with your optometrist. Fluorescent lights are notoriously bad lighting for a workshop, because they diffuse light and make it difficult to see work, as discussed in the section "About Light" in Chapter 1. One of the best sources of artificial lighting for carving is the filament bulb reading lamp, but one of the less obvious, nonetheless present, hazards is electrocution from accidentally breaking the light bulb with a chisel or a mallet. Sometimes it is too easy for us to get so "carried away" that we forget where the light is and an accident occurs. It is important, then, to ensure that the brightness strength of the light bulb is sufficient that you don't need to have it so close as to become a danger.

Lighting is also a potential source for burns. For example, halogen lighting is an efficient source of light energy, but it generates considerable heat—so much so that it can be a source of skin burns if not used with great care. The intensity of this light may also damage your eyes if they are not protected.

---

tracing—a small piece of adhesive tape is useful. Blue—or black—ink carbon paper is ideal for lighter-colored woods, and white carbon, if you can find it, is perfect for darker colors.

If the wood surface is rough or open grained, this method may not be particularly satisfactory.

Tracing from a Template

If a template is used (as discussed in Chapter 5, for example), it will be necessary to use a very fine-tipped pencil such as a ½₂-in (0.5mm) mechanical pencil, ensuring that the lead is as close as possible to the edge of the template where it meets the wood surface. Otherwise the pattern will be oversized on the wood.

Freehand Drawing

Clearly there is some level of drawing skill needed for the aspiring woodcarver. Have available an eraser—preferably a clear gum variety, because colored rubber erasers will leave marks on your wood. Try a variety of pencils. White and red are very useful in a hard crayon variety that can be sharpened. Graphite pencils can be hard to see, but fine-tipped felt pens are a handy substitute.

Finishes

There are many and varied commercially available finishes for your carvings. Whichever you choose, there are some principles that might ensure you use the best kind for your work:

Whatever you do, experiment on a scrap of the same wood as the carving (even carving part of it so that you simulate real conditions) with whatever finish you want to use. This can save many a tragic outcome.

An untreated surface may attract a lot of dust and become soiled easily. A considerable overall surface area of wood is exposed to the atmosphere by a carved surface and this adds to the likelihood of dust collection.

A very shiny surface will reflect a lot more light that a dull one. If the area is carved and shiny, you can expect that much of the shadow will be eliminated, and there may be a mass of reflected light that spoils the overall intended image. A duller surface finish may be more appropriate than a shiny one.

Shaping a Gouge for Effective Use

In Harder Woods

Consider that we have a chisel that has a long, skinny bevel; then the thickness of the steel towards and at the cutting edge will be quite thin. When we push that thin cutting edge into harder wood, we are likely to damage—chip, serrate, or break—the cutting edge because it is so weak. What we need to do is to strengthen the steel formation at the cutting edge. A strengthened edge will allow us to cut into hard wood without damage.

What we have to do is make the steel thicker to make it stronger. The way to make the steel thicker is to alter the shape of the cutting edge. There are two ways we can do this:

1 We can alter the curve of the bevel to make it more acute.

To make the steel thicker and therefore stronger, the bevel needs to be "rounded off." Unfortunately this can have a detrimental effect. While increasing the strength of the cutting edge, it also increases the angle of approach of the chisel into the wood, making the chisel more difficult to use.

2 We can grind on what is called a "secondary bevel" rather than alter the curve of the bevel. The secondary bevel is on the top side of the tool.

This can be done in two ways:

A Instead of rounding off the bevel shape, a "deliberate" and defined bevel can be added to the one already there, the end result being the same as rounding off, as above.

B Rather than adding the bevel to the one already there, place the additional bevel on the topside of the tool—this increases the strength without altering the behavior of the tool.

An additional benefit is that the tool can be used more easily upside down for creating beads or their equivalent. The secondary bevel doesn't need to be very large. You can experiment; however, about $\frac{1}{16}$ in (1 to 1½mm) is generally sufficient.

In Softer Woods

Basically this process is the opposite of that with harder woods. It is always wise to experiment with these bevel shapes. However, what you will most likely find is that long, thin bevels are best in woods like lime and white beech.

The flatter the better, although a very slightly(almost nondetectably) convex bevel will generally outperform an absolutely flat bevel, unless you are trying to produce a completely flat surface. Because the slight curve in the bevel will push the tool out of the wood—requiring you to maintain a slight counterpressure to keep the chisel in the wood—this effectively increases your control.

The Oiling Process

If a natural oil, such as tung, walnut, almond, or orange, is used for the surface finish, it will soak in, given time, and will become dry and very bland. Enough coats should be rubbed in to seal the pores and build up a smooth surface, which will eventually take on a low luster when the oiled surface is dry. Oiling is a process that takes many applications and can be time-consuming, although the results can also be very pleasing. The oil you choose may also darken the wood considerably (as does tung oil).

If you apply a wax directly to untreated wood, it may soak in and require a large number of applications to be effective. The same of course may apply to oils you might try.

If you apply a wax, do so with only a small amount with each application. Too much applied at once may mean you end up with a tacky mess that is difficult to clean up.

Sealing the Surface

Experiment by sealing the surface first with a sanding sealer or something that is similar, and then by applying oils or waxes. In this way a better result may be achieved more quickly.

Shellac is an excellent sealer as a base for oils and particularly waxes. But you will want to keep in mind that shellac will darken with time. Eventually—this could take decades—the shellac may perish and become cracked on the surface.

Danger of Fire

The most common cause of fire in the workshop is from flammable liquids, electrical fault, or spontaneous combustion.

Electrical Hazards

Eliminating the possibility of electrical fault is best dealt with by a safety check from a competent electrician. There are some things that you can check yourself, and these include identifying frayed power leads, broken plugs or switches, and potential overloads on circuits. Also protect against electrical hazard by installing ground-fault circuit interrupters (GFCIs) for all power outlets and equipment in your working area.

Wood Dust

Wood dust in machinery is a possible source of fire, so a clean environment helps. Making sure a plug is in a socket properly and a switch is turned ON or OFF and not sitting halfway may avoid problems. Intermittent current across terminals may start a fire.

Fire Extinquisher

Check with your insurance company or local fire station as to the best kind of extinguisher to have handy on the workshop wall. Also, keeping a fire blanket on hand is an excellent precaution.

Remember to place an extinguisher or blanket near where you will most often be, and not so you have to walk across a room on fire to get to it. Near an exit, for example, might be the right place.

Flammable Liquids

Store flammable liquids away from heat such as radiators and pilot lights, and as a rule it is best not to allow smoking in your workshop. The most common flammable liquids in your workshop would be turpentine, methylated spirit, acetone, and kerosene. Also place any of these types of flammable liquids out of the reach of children, and make sure their container lids are airtight and are not leaking fumes. Never use any of these liquids to accelerate the fire in a workshop woodstove, as you may well have a severe or fatal accident.

Some of the most harmless of ingredients can turn out to be the most surprisingly dangerous. Nut oils are typical. Tung (from the Chinese tung tree), linseed (from the flax plant), walnut, almond, pecan, olive, and other cooking oils are among those that may spontaneously ignite if the conditions are right. Never leave oily rags or paper towels scrunched up in the waste bin in your workshop. Store them in a metal container out of potential harm's way and dispose of them properly at the end of each day, washing them before throwing them out, or if you have them in any significant volume, disposing of them as hazardous waste.

Gluing Wood

Gluing is not a common practice in woodcarving, the majority of circumstances being laminating pieces of wood into boards or blocks, and repair work. There is a large range of glues to choose from, and in all cases the instructions on the labels should be followed.

It is important to remember that most glues are toxic to one degree or another, the least toxic being the water-based glues such as hide glues, polyvinyl acetate (PVA), acrylic copolymers, and casein glues, which may irritate the skin or cause upset from inhalation or ingestion.

An excellent glue for immediate repair to a carving in progress is "instant glue," or Super Glue™, which is available in one part or two parts including an accelerator. Unfortunately these are cyanoacrylate glues and are extremely hazardous. While moderately toxic by skin contact, they can instantly glue skin together, sometimes requiring surgery, and can cause extreme irritation to eyes. Always use these glues with great care, and your instant repair jobs should be outstanding and hazard free.

Avoid Contact and Resin Glues

Contact adhesives would not be used very often, if at all, in a woodcarving sense; however, it is as well to know that they are highly flammable, and if they contain hexane may cause nerve damage; also other solvents in them may cause irritation to skin, lungs, or stomach.

Often used for larger surface areas, resorcinol and urea formaldehyde resin glues are highly toxic by eye contact and inhalation, and can be irritating to the skin. Formaldehyde is a known human carcinogen, and sanding dust may release formaldehyde. Epoxy glues, also popular for larger surface areas, can cause skin irritation, asthma, and other lung conditions.

Use Water-Based Glues

To avoid these hazards, use water-based glues whenever possible, avoid glues with formaldehyde, wear gloves when using epoxy, formaldehyde resin, or solvent-based glues, and ensure good ventilation of your workshop. Be careful of fire with solvent-based glues, never allow smoking, and do not use near an open flame.

Machinery Hazards

Each particular machine will have its own peculiar hazards and these will most likely be discussed in the manufacturer's instruction manual that came with it.

Electrocution, injury such as dismemberment and eye scratches, noise-related injury (hearing disorders), and dust inhalation are the main hazards you will face. It is imperative that you read and follow the instruction manuals for your machinery, and that you maintain machinery in good working order. This is simply common sense.

What may not be quite so obvious are things such as the location of power outlets and switches for machinery and other power tools. Main ON/OFF switches at power outlets should be out of reach to children. There should be a panic—or emergency—OFF switch readily accessible to all, including children. If your chain saw needs fuel, store that elsewhere, out of reach, and in a cool dry place. Don't have power cords and power connectors lying on the floor.

Blunt band-saw blades are a cause of accidents, so keep your blades well maintained. Numbness of the fingers can be the permanent result of damage from vibrating tools like chain saws and sanders, so avoid prolonged exposure.

Long hair, neckties, loose clothing, long jewelry, and necklaces (including neck strings with your glasses attached) are serious machinery hazards. If your long hair gets caught in a drill press, you can easily be scalped.

Make sure switches are fully on/off. A switch that is partially off can easily flip back into the ON position, and a serious accident may result. Always disconnect machinery from its power source when it is not being used.

Using Paints and Pigments

It is not often, but it is possible, that the carver will want to color wood or its surface with various pigments. The same comments apply to pigments as to wood dust. Whatever you do, unless you know absolutely that a pigment is free of toxic effect, never ingest it, breathe it in, or let it settle on your skin. Some of the chemicals that appear to be harmless pigments can cause toxic reactions that result in mental or physical illness such as cancer or death—even from one exposure!

Avoid using pigments or paints in any situation where the carving might end up in children's hands (e.g., toys), especially as they are likely to put it in their mouth.

Use Ready-Made Paint

If the carving is to be painted, avoid mixing your own paint. Ready-made paint is much safer for obvious reasons. Avoid inhalation of the solvents in paint or varnish by using them in well-ventilated areas and using respirators where appropriate; also do not eat, drink, or smoke in a paint area. Wear gloves and goggles to avoid skin contact and eye damage. Solvent vapors can be extremely irritating. Also be especially careful using aerosol cans; keep these well out of reach of children.

Paint Stripping

Removing old paint and varnish to expose a fresh surface for carving may introduce you to a wide variety of hazards. Sanding will generate dust that must not be breathed in, so a nose and mouth mask is essential.

Removing stains with bleaches could expose you to oxalic acid, caustic soda, or hydrogen peroxide. Paint strippers contain a wide variety of solvents, including benzene, toluene, alcohol, methyl chloride, and glycol ethers. Methyl chloride, for example, may change heartbeat rhythms and cause fatal heart attacks, and is a suspected carcinogen. If mixtures of chlorine bleach and ammonia are inhaled, death may result.

A popular method of removing paint is to use a blowtorch or heat gun. These burn and vaporize paint, which may in turn cause lead poisoning if the fumes are inhaled.

If you find that it is necessary to use paint and varnish strippers, the following safety precautions are essential:

✻ Wear gloves, respirator, eye goggles, and apron

✻ Conduct the activity outside, or ensure excellent ventilation

✻ Do not smoke, or use any solvents near exposed flame, including pilot lights on heaters

✻ Ensure that there is instant access to running water (preferably a shower) or at best a bucket of water to wash spills from your skin, and eyewash for emergency treatment

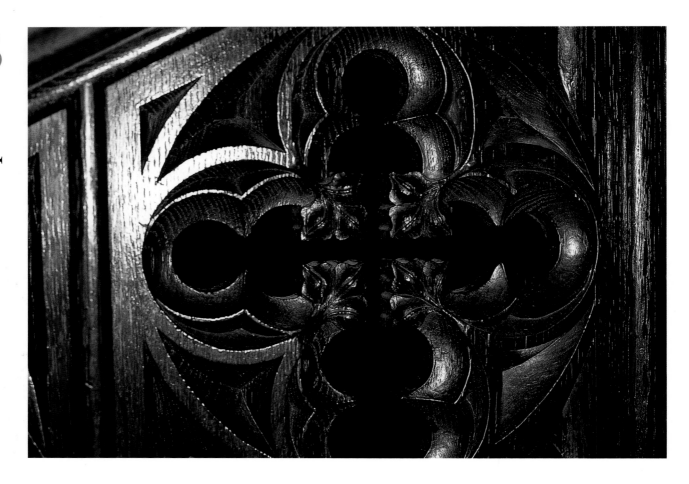

chapter 3

CAN I CARVE IT?

*Suitability
of Woods
for Carving*

Among the woodcarving fraternity, the most often asked questions relate to wood. Which one should I use? Can I carve it? Where do you get it? Is it any good? How much does it cost?

In this chapter we look at wood from the point of view of the novice woodcarver. It is not the intention to present a technical treatise on wood—there is plenty of material available elsewhere. It is my intention to answer a variety of commonly asked questions about wood as they relate to the carving of it.

The questions are as endless as the subject matter: Does it matter if wood is "wet"? What will happen if wood dries out? Why are European, English, and American linden (widely known as lime) considered so good? For what? Can I carve wood so dense it sinks in water? What is "against the grain"? How do I know by sight and feel that I will have difficulty carving a piece of wood? How can I work out what a piece of wood is good for? How should I store wood?

It is a topic that could be a lifetime study, and even then there would be many unanswered questions about so many different species. Wood can also be one of the most perplexing subjects. However, like most things, it can be reduced to a set of basic guidelines which, once understood, can take care of many major challenges.

To understand some of the basics about wood from a carving point of view, we need to break the subject down into the components that affect us the most.

Before we do that, though, let us start by saying that if all the factors that affect successful woodcarving are taken into account, then any wood can be used to carve at least something, irrespective of its species. It is just that some species will be more difficult to carve than others, and some more appropriate than others for a particular application. The first concept that requires general acceptance is that there are no absolute rules about wood. It's a bit like the weather: Every time the wind blows it's a bit different from last time. There are patterns and generalizations, but nothing hard and fast. The same tree will yield wood with different behavior patterns depending on where in the tree it came from. The wood's density (weight per unit volume), the shape of the cells it is made of, and the "lie" of the cells will all contribute to its properties. The shape of the bevel on your chisel will influence the general behavior of the wood, as will the ambient humidity level. The variables are extensive, and so, therefore, are the outcomes.

To be able to decide which wood is for what carving, or what carving is for which wood, we need to know the right questions to ask. In order to put it all into some kind of perspective, it is easiest to examine the most common wood characteristics you will need to take into consideration, and then apply them to some specific and common species.

The Characteristics of Wood

The concept of "equilibrium" is the crux of the answer to the question "Which wood?" We are speaking of the equilibrium between the person carving, the tool being used, the design being created, and the chosen wood.

This equilibrium is affected by many factors that influence the appropriateness of a particular species for a particular project. These factors include color, cell characteristics, what part of the tree the wood came from (e.g., root, branch, trunk), density, and grain characteristics.

In addition, we must not lose sight of the fact that it is the chisels that cut into the wood, and therefore

"Wood comes from trees. This is the most important fact to remember in understanding the nature of wood. Whatever qualities or shortcomings wood possesses are traceable to the tree whence it came. Wood evolved as a functional tissue of plants rather than as a material designed to satisfy the needs of woodworkers. Thus, knowing wood as it grows in nature is basic to working successfully with it."

—Bruce Hoadley
Understanding Wood,
Taunton Press, 1980

they play a very significant role in our equation of equilibrium between the wood we are working and the subject matter. So this chapter must be read in context with the side boxes on managing your tools in Chapter 2, "Which Tool?" because in the final analysis the chisel must be sharpened to suit the medium (and the subject) for which it will be used. You should also refer to Chapter 4, "Of Course You Can Draw!" where there is a discussion about choosing suitable carving subject matter.

Of all the characteristics of wood, the two most important for influencing a choice are:

CELL CHARACTERISTICS—Cell size, shape, wall thickness, and layout will help determine the amount of detail and the kind of design the wood can tolerate.

COLOR (including multiple colors)—Color will help determine the wood's ability to show off shadows, apart from any other aesthetic factors that may be relevant. This is a particularly important consideration, and reference should be made to Chapter 1 for more detail.

Other factors that will have an influence are age of the wood, its moisture level, whether it is sapwood or heartwood, or whether it comes from a branch or a trunk or a root.

Each of these key attributes is, for all intents and purposes, equally important as the other. They are certainly mutually inclusive, and interdependent. So where to start? There is no one answer that makes more sense than the other, except for three things:

- ✳ Ease
- ✳ Convenience
- ✳ Effectiveness

Easy to carve, convenient to purchase, and with the capacity to support the desired result.

By now you will be realizing that there are so many factors involved in the carving process that there is plenty of room for confusion. At this point, then, we need to stop and take in the apparent magnitude of the task. "Apparent" is the key word, because in the end you will find that as your experience with different tools, designs, and woods grows, your learning curve will also grow. This growth will be at such a fast rate you will become very familiar very quickly with a vast array of combinations and permutations of all the aspects of the craft. Eventually your knowledge of wood will become instinctive.

It is important to accept at this stage that the only obstacle to your success is experience. And the only obstacle to experience is experimentation. And that is the most important ingredient of all. Experiment, experiment, experiment! That gives you experience, and, just as important, many and varied experiences, not just the same thing over and over again. You will notice that we did not say practice, practice, practice! But experiment, experiment, experiment! There is no point whatsoever in subscribing solely to the theory that practice makes perfect. Not in woodcarving. Why?

3-1. Typical cell shapes found in wood. The nature of the cells and their configuration give the wood its characteristics.

Because no two pieces of wood are the same, and no two sets of carving conditions are the same—your own mental disposition may be one of the greatest variables. Experimentation will give you experience, which will give you versatility, and versatility will enable you to satisfy a wider variety of demands, therefore making you more successful.

Since we are intending to experiment, then, we need to develop a mindset that will enable us to sustain an inquiring mind that will in turn enable us to develop versatility in the future. So here we have our formula for successful carving: the establishment of a woodcarving mindset that thrives on experimentation to achieve equilibrium.

To get things going, a list of things to think about first is presented below. They are in alphabetical order so as not to suggest that any one is more important than another, and they all relate to the spectrum of questions from "Can I carve it?" to "What should I use it for?" Add these tems to the database of your new woodcarving mindset:

BRITTLE wood will break easily and is generally not a proposition for fine details in carvings. Jelutong (not readily available in North America) can be brittle. So can American walnut and Australian scented rose mahogany, if you want to maintain fine, sharp edges in your design. Western red cedar is also brittle, can be spongy, and splits easily. European pear wood, American basswood, and willow are generally the opposite of brittle. If the design changes direction a lot, this indicates it might be best to use a fine, straight-grained wood that does not chip or break easily.

CELLS are the fundamental structural component of wood. Typical shapes are shown in 3-1. They come in an endless variety of size, shape, wall thickness, and configuration, each species having its own "signature" by which it can be identified. It is the configuration and subsequent mass of the cells that gives each species its characteristic properties. When you carve wood, you are cutting through these cells, and the ability of the wood to cope with carving will depend on the nature of the cells (as well as your skill and the tools themselves). If you imagine the cell to be like a tube, when you carve it you are either cutting along it and opening up the side of the cell, or cutting across the end and exposing it as a more or less round hole. The size and shape of the resulting

3-3. *This carving from St. Andrew's Cathedral in Sydney, Australia, is from brown oak, stained even darker. Shadows are lost, the darker the wood.*

3-2. *(Above left) Australian gidgee is one of the densest woods of the world, but can be carved very effectively. This carving, "The Gidgee Bird," is courtesy of Mr. Bill Shean.*

3-4. *(Above right) If this carving in similar oak in St. Andrew's Cathedral in Inverness, Scotland, were stained darker, the pattern in the central shield would never be seen.*

opening will dictate how the wood reacts to the cutting process. If the result is a lot of large openings in cells that have weak, thin walls, then the carving will most likely be messy and "broken up," as might happen with balsa wood or cork oak.

CLIMATE is an important issue for woodcarvings. When wood is "dry," or seasoned, it has a water content that suits its environment. If this is tropical, for example, it will be significantly higher than if in an arid location. When a carving (or any wooden item, for that matter) is moved from one locality to another, it will expand or contract according to the moisture loss or uptake from the ambient atmosphere. This movement may mean it will be damaged permanently. Air conditioning is often very drying, as are room heaters (particularly gas and wood fires), and these should be considered as threats to the integrity of the wood you are using. Eucalypts tend to move a lot, whereas less dense and more uniformly grained woods like cedar do not.

CLOSE- (also known as FINE-) grained wood is wood that has cells that are generally small and fine and laid close together to make a densely packed mass. Close-grained wood is often relatively heavy or dense (weight per unit volume). A close-grained wood that is relatively soft, like European linden (lime) or white beech, will normally support a significant amount of fine detail carving. lignumvitae, wattle (Australian gidgee), and ebony, on the other hand, while each also being very close-grained, are so dense that carving is considerably more difficult, but not impossible. The dry density of gidgee is about 2340 lb/yd^3 (1330kg/m^3). The carving in 3-2 is carved from wattle (Australian gidgee).

COLOR is important if the design has a lot of shadows. A light-colored wood will generally show off shadows better than a dark color. Compare the woods and carvings in 3-3 and 3-4. Quite often color is important to the design of the particular carving, and unfortunately quite often the best carving woods for the design and the application are the wrong color. The best—usually meaning the easiest—woods for carving tend to be rather bland and characterless. They are figure-less, meaning not particularly interesting, straight-grained, and generally very plain in color, such as beech, kauvula from Fiji, or yellow such as devil tree (cheesewood) and jelutong from Papua New Guinea and Indonesia, respectively, or light brown like bollywood from northern Australia.

CRISP wood is wood that cuts cleanly and accurately the first time. You put a chisel through it, and you get precisely what you want when and where you want it. Provided your chisel is sharp, jelutong from Indonesia is like this. So is American black walnut (its relatively high silica content will blunt your tool quickly) or fine English oak. Poor-quality jelutong can also be spongy and flaky, and poor-quality English oak coarse and likely to split along the fibers.

DENSITY is the measure of weight per unit volume and is expressed in pounds per cubic yard (lb/yd^3) or kilograms per cubic meter (kg/m^3). Density will vary according to moisture content, and may be expressed as "average dry density" or "average green density." Dense woods generally "move" (swell and shrink depending on moisture content) more than less dense woods, so if you carve green dense wood, it may well "check" (crack) if you are not very careful. To reduce this possibility, keep "wet" wood you are carving in a cool, dry place, well out of wind and direct sunlight, and keep a moist cloth over the carving to slow down the drying-out process. Sudden drying can cause cracks to appear. You may wet the surface with an atomizer. If you do apply moisture, watch for mold growth that may stain the wood. Wash with an anti-mold bathroom liquid. On the other hand, sometimes if the wood splits it can be an advantage if you want to simulate age, as in 3-5.

If the carving is to be highly polished, then a fine-grained, dense wood might be best. If the carving is for a decorative wall plaque, you will not want a wood so heavy it will fall off the wall. If the carving is for furniture, the wood will need to be strong and durable and denser than the wall plaque.

If you are carving a large work in most hardwoods (e.g., New Zealand black maire), it will be necessary to alter the angle of the bevel on your chisel to reduce the likelihood of serrating or chipping its cutting edge. Try

3-5. Checks can help to simulate age, like this white beech figure inspired by a twelfth-century chess pawn.

increasing the angle anything up to 10 degrees if chipping occurs. Regrind progressively until you find the best angle that interferes the least with the cutting action of the tool. An alternative is to put a secondary bevel on the inside of the tool, thereby increasing the strength of the cutting edge without altering the behavior of the chisel. (Refer to the side boxes in Chapter 2 for a detailed discussion of the process of sharpening.)

"DRY" is a term that refers to wood when it is "seasoned." Seasoned wood is wood that has reached a moisture (water) content that is approximately equal to the ambient moisture content in the atmosphere. Therefore a wood that is "dry" in Bangkok will be "wetter" than a wood that is "dry" in Toronto. They will not be identical because ambient moisture content can vary dramatically and quickly, whereas wood moisture content will vary much more slowly. Once the moisture content of the wood is down to a "dry" level, it will rise only marginally and slowly. It is the drying out and the occasional marginal reconstitution of moisture that cause wood to *move*. A "dry" wood may have a moisture content anywhere between 10 and 20 percent.

FIGURE refers to the appearance of the configuration of the cells of the wood. It is the pattern in the wood made by the cells, their shape and color, and the direction in which they lie. Figure may be sometimes referred to as swirl, curly, wavy, fiddleback, straight, interlocked, indented, mottled, dimpled, roey, striped, ribboned, bird's-eye, quilted, blistered, knotty (pin, loose, spike, tight, intergrown, encased), or pigmented. The figure in the wood can adversely affect the way it behaves. Knots can be difficult to handle, and because these are generally fairly hard they may cause chipping of your chisels. Wavy grain around them can help make the wood prone to tearing and chipping. Heavily striped woods can have different density, hardness, and grain strength in the different colors. When

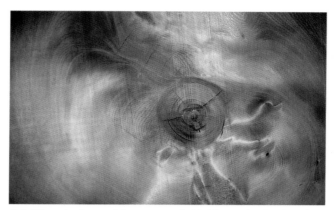

3-6. There is plenty of figure around this Huon pine knot. This piece of wood would be quite difficult to carve.

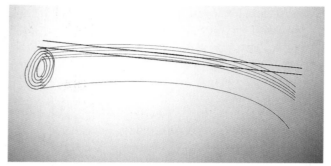

3-8. Grain direction depends on how the plank is cut from the original log.

a wavy characteristic is present, generally the coarser the fibers the greater the likelihood of breakage. The Huon pine in 3-6 has plenty of figure.

"FLAKY" means that when you carve into it, the wood comes off in layers and not necessarily how you intended. Bundles of cells are lifted off "in the flat" (as opposed to "along the grain," which is more a splitting action). Close-grained wood like European linden (lime) can be flaky, as can be white cypress. If you encounter flaky wood, you need to be sure your tools are very, very sharp, and preferably have a long, thin bevel so as to reduce the likelihood of too much wood accidentally being removed at one time. Flaky woods are generally fine for carvings that don't have great amounts of detail, although linden, if treated correctly can support some amazing works of art.

"GRAIN" is a much-used word that is loosely used to refer to such a wide variety of visual and textural effects in wood that it is a generic word for anything.

GRAIN DIRECTION is also a loosely used term referring to the angle of the lie of the wood cells relative to

3-7. The cut to the left was with the grain. The cut to the right in this jelutong is against the grain and results in fracturing.

the direction a chisel is being pushed. If the chisel cuts (pushes) easily through the wood, it is generally going "with the grain" (it could also be going across it), and if the wood fractures, the chisel is generally going "against the grain," (see 3-7). It is very important and fundamental to carving that the concepts of "with" and "against" the grain are understood. This understanding will save a considerable amount of breakage and unnecessary damage to your work. Consider the log of wood in 3-8, and follow each of the statements referring to it:

1 Imagine that the growth rings represent a set of tubes, each made of cells, each tube one inside the other, running the full length of the log.

2 The two thick parallel lines represent a plank that has been cut out of the log at the sawmill.

3 Now, if you push a gouge (or hand plane, scraper, or carpenter's chisel or any other cutting tool) along the topside of our plank from right to left, your tool will be traveling with the grain as it moves towards the center of the log. Because it will be sliding off the ends of the fibers, at the center it will be moving neither with nor against the grain, because the fibers are laid parallel to the surface of the plank. As you continue to the left it will be moving against the grain, because it will be digging into the ends of the fibers. A fiber is, strictly speaking, a long, thin cell like the one shown in 3-1. The word is used very loosely and often in the context of "grain."

4 On the underside of the plank, if you move your tool in the same direction as the topside, the opposite will occur, because the fiber ends are pointing in the opposite direction.

Therefore, just because the grain is in one direction in one part of the wood you might be carving doesn't automatically mean that anywhere on a plank the grain direction will be the same. It depends entirely on how the piece of wood was cut out of the log.

"HARD WOOD" refers to density as far as carving is concerned. In botanical terms, a "hardwood" is a species that produces seeds that form inside a ripening fruit. They are known generally as "angiosperms," and in this botanical context "hard" has nothing to do with the wood's relative density.

KNOTS represent the growth of a new branch from within the tree (they start to grow from the center or pith) and they can be a major problem for the carver. In the majority of cases, they are surrounded by wavy, often interlocked layers of cells, of different densities, and are not able to support regular and predictable chisel work. If you are selecting wood from a log or tree, knotty areas are easy to identify because they will be where the branches appear from the bark, as in 3-9. Or, in the case of 3-10, the wavy texture of the bark is a sure indication of possible knot presence and wavy cell structure underneath.

OPEN- (also known as COARSE-) grained wood is generally the opposite of fine-grained. Typical woods are chestnut, fir, meranti, oak, and wenge. Woods with this characteristic are generally not good for most carvings, unless the project is not particularly detailed, such as a bulky sculpture. They would not be considered as good for decorative furniture work. One benefit of open-grained woods is that they often glue well, because the glue more easily penetrates the surface so if you do break part of the carving off it can generally be repaired easily. Always be sure with grainy woods like this that your design is not presenting a weakness along the grain, such as an animal's leg that might break off if any stress were placed across it. The lie of the cells should be along the leg for maximum strength.

REACTION WOOD forms in trees that lean (see 3-11). The curving sweep of the tree means that wood under compression (and highly unpredictable) will be found inside. The pith may be quite off center and the growth rings very unevenly placed in the log as a result. In this the wood that is bent is also known as "tension wood."

RECYCLING WOOD is often a popular way to recover high-quality wood to save cost or for aesthetic or nos-

3-9. The branch starts at the center of the host wood, so the "knot" goes all the way to the middle.

3-10. Wavy bark often means interlocked wavy grain underneath.

3-11. Bends in logs generally mean problems—there may be a lot of inside tension and unpredictable behavior as a result.

talgic reasons. There are, however, significant dangers that must be taken into consideration, the most common being hidden nails and screws that will cause extreme damage to your tools. The piece of Douglas fir in 3-12 has the added disadvantage of a large knot, which may also cause chisel damage due to its relative hardness.

SOFT WOOD refers to density as far as carving is generally concerned. In botanical terms, a "softwood" is a species that produces an uncovered seed most often in a cone type of structure (conifer) and fits into the category known as "gymnosperms"; and in this botanical context the term "soft" has nothing to do with the wood's relative density.

"SPLITTING" is a term that seems to relate to a number of conditions. When wood dries out, it tends to shrink as the moisture evaporates from the cells and their walls begin to collapse. As they separate from one another, cracks appear; these are also sometimes known as *checks*. Sometimes the cracks are inside the wood and are not seen until it is too late—they are known as "internal checks," or "heart checks." No doubt there are other names as well—unsuspecting carvers who have had an unscheduled repair job on their hands would certainly call them a few different things!

SPONGY WOOD is as the name implies—the wood is too soft and squashy to cut very cleanly, particularly when a chisel is pushed through it vertically down the end grain. Malaysian kauri can be like this, as can Monterey pine and Canadian redwood. A finely honed and thin bevel is best, to keep this as under control as possible. A design that has a lot of end-grain carving (e.g., wood blocks for printing) or one that is to be undercut a lot should be avoided if spongy wood is to be carved.

TEARING of the fibers is a symptom either of a blunt tool that pushes at the fibers and cells and breaks them

3-12. Recycling wood can have many hidden dangers. (Refer also to the side boxes in Chapter 2, "Which Tool?")

rather than cutting straight through them or of a very coarse wood that will also split easily. A coarse wood is not necessarily only one that has fibers spread wide apart like wenge, but more one that doesn't want to be cut cleanly, like Douglas fir—at least not with hand tools like woodcarving chisels. It might cut very well with high-speed tools, as on a lathe or an electric planer. In other words, it will give way under pressure from a machine, but with a mere mortal, not so! If the carving has large areas without detailed patterns that need to be completely unblemished for best results, a wood that scrapes or sands cleanly without any tear-out might be best.

WAXY WOOD lubricates itself as you cut it, and with a sharp tool it will polish itself as it goes. Some examples are wattle (Australian gidgee), linden (lime), and ebony. Each of these woods is also fairly fine-grained and is therefore conducive to good and easy polishing—there are no gaps to be filled to get a smooth surface. Lignumvitae has been used for propeller shaft bearings, and tallowwood for draw runners, because they are naturally greasy. If the carving is for the exterior of a boat, it will need to be weather resistant. Waxy woods, like white beech, can be good for decking because they resist water penetration. Care needs to be taken when gluing waxy woods—wash the surface with methylated spirits or acetone for best results.

WET WOOD—also called GREEN—has just been cut from the tree and has not had a chance to dry out. Its moisture (water) content may be anywhere from 20 percent upwards as high as 40 percent. As wood dries, its cell walls shrink, and it will "move" (contract). Some woods contract a lot, up to five percent, and some very little. Textbooks on wood technology often include charts on woods and their "average dry" and "average green" densities, as well as their shrinkage rates, which will give an indication of their suitability as carving woods before they "season."

Some Carving Woods

In order to see some of the characteristics in context, some woods that you might want to carve are described below. See also the Appendix for a list of the common and botanical names of wood.

Beech

A fine- to-medium–close grain of medium density—average dry density of 880 lb/yd³ (500kg/m³)—generally straight and predictable cell structure; easy to carve and can take on a silky, waxy look off the chisel; can be flaky and will split if cut in the wrong direction but generally behaves very well; will support reasonably fine detail, but fibers do not always cling together like linden (lime); takes a long time to season; pale uninteresting gray color, sometimes with a wide pink stripe tinge, but shows off shadows well.

Honduras Mahogany

A good all-rounder for carving. Takes moderate to high detail, can be subject to wavy and interlocked grain but is generally straight and predictable. If too dry, it tends to be crumbly and will split if mishandled. Surface dryness can be reduced significantly and the wood made much more manageable if sprayed with an atomizer.

Jarrah

Native to southwestern Australia, jarrah has an average dry density of about 1440 lb/yd³ (820kg/m³) and is a relatively coarsely grained wood with slightly interlocked grain. It is a general-construction wood, was commonly used for railway sleepers and fence posts, and was exported to the UK for use as road paving. It is now commonly used for furniture in Australia. It is reasonably hard, splinters easily, but cuts cleanly with a sharp, well-controlled chisel, cutting along the grain. It will tear out cutting across the grain, as will most Australian eucalypts.

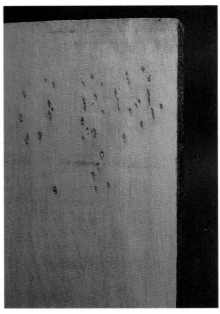

3-13. Sap pockets in jelutong are often discovered only after carving has commenced. Many species have hidden gum veins, particularly eucalyptus.

Jelutong

Jelutong has an average dry density of about 700 lb/yd³ (400kg/m³) with characteristic gum pockets that can be several inches deep and not always apparent on the surface (see 3-13). With care, crisp and finely edged carving can be achieved with jelutong; however, it is too fragile to be suitable for carvings with sharp edges and steep rises. While its lack of strength makes it generally unsuitable for such carvings, its crispness and low density makes it ideal for large picture frames that might be gessoed and gilded. It is also suitable for rocking horses, door cores, and drawing boards. Because it is soft and coarse it has little substance and does not easily give a crisp finish. The ends of the fibers are easily raised when applying water or spirit-based finishes, and therefore need scraping or papering to clean them up.

Meranti

Meranti is known as white lauan and less in Australia generically as Pacific maple. It is commonly referred to as light red meranti. The average dry density is between 700 and about 1130 lb/yd³ (400 and 640kg/m³). Meranti machines well and is generally used for light construction purposes such as doors, windows, architraves, and skirting boards. It has a coarse interlocked grain that tends to be stringy and spongy, and demands a sharp chisel to avoid its characteristic woolly tearing.

Merbau

Merbau from Malaysia is also known as kwila from New Guinea. Merbau has an average dry density of 1500 lb/yd³ (850kg/m³). This is a slightly interlocked grainy and greasy wood with a highly irritant sanding dust, and is used for furniture, paneling, and boat building as well as carving. It has a yellow dye in it capable of staining fabrics and concrete. The grainy nature of the wood makes it unsuitable for detailed carvings, and as with most grainy woods it is best to test the design in the wood first before committing yourself to carving it.

Mountain Ash

Has an average dry density of about 1180 lb/yd³ (670kg/m³) and is commonly used for furniture and boat building. It is not often carved, but it has characteristics that cover a large number of woods, so it is worth including in this study. Any woods that are good for steam bending, like mountain ash, generally have a long fiber, which is conducive to bending. Short-fiber woods tend to fracture more easily. This characteristic can also make the carving process harder. In the case of mountain ash, it is a hard wood with long, wavy, sometimes interlocked fibers that tend to want to grab the chisel. There can be a lot of tear, and it is easily splintered.

Poplar

Is a commonly carved wood, which behaves in much the same way as meranti.

Rimu

Rimu has an average dry density of about 1060 lb/yd³ (600kg/m³), and is a fine, even, straight-grained textured wood. Rimu is typically used for flooring, furniture, paneling, and plywood; it is good for steam bending. It has long, stringy fibers that tend to grab the chisel (like mountain ash), and this can make it difficult to exit the wood easily. It cuts fairly cleanly along the grain, but if you are not careful the long, stringy fibers may splinter.

Rose Mahogany

Is commonly known as (scented) rosewood, and the average dry density is about 1270 lb/yd³ (720kg/m³). This is used for furniture and paneling and tends to be flaky and brittle where sharp rises occur, so the design needs to take this into consideration. The grain is wavy, so to help stop it from breaking you need to chisel it diagonally across the grain or along the waves, within reason, changing direction frequently. A very sharp, slim chisel such as a fishtail with a long bevel, giving a low approach to the wood, is best. Take fine shavings for best results.

Wattle (Australian gidgee)

An Australian inland desert wattle that weighs about 2340 lb/yd³ (1330kg/m³). It is basically very difficult to do much with it when seasoned, but is generally workable when wet and can be carved with a correctly beveled chisel. Very fine-grained and has a waxy look off the chisel.

chapter 4

OF COURSE
YOU CAN DRAW!

Drawing and Modeling for Wood-carving

It is important to keep the drawing part of woodcarving in perspective. To say it is essential to have drawing skills in order to be a successful woodcarver isn't really true. Anything can be copied. After all, the woodcarving is the end result and that is what will be judged. The means of getting there, many and varied, will be specifically influenced by the way the carver wants to do it, and will be in turn influenced by what the carver's particular skills are. Drawing the object or design in the first place may or may not be a part of those means, skills, or desires.

The absolute "purist" will most likely draw first, then make a working model, and then do the carving. The opposite-type person will most likely just go and carve. If the end results are equally substantive, then the approach is more one of academic interest than of practical relevance. What you and I want to determine for the present, however, are the inherent advantages of being able to draw, and how it might be best to draw so that you can easily carve the subject some other time.

We will also examine some reasons for modeling the subject and some of the techniques surrounding the making of those models.

Taking the most pragmatic approach to the whole subject, then, I would start with the simplest question: Why draw at all? There is only one reason in the context of woodcarving, and that is to create a record.

During this record-creating process, we also sort out in our mind those characteristics that we consider important to the subject, and more important, our interpretation of them, from a reproduction point of view.

And therein lies the secret to the whole of the recording process. We are setting out to create a record, but to do it we need to interpret what our senses detect, and to do that successfully we need to be sure that we develop the ability to detect information in the first place.

This is just as if the woodworking teacher were working with a student who was totally blind. The teacher instructs the student to complete a certain procedure, which the blind student declares to be wrong. The student, alerting the teacher, who admits his error, had been reading Braille construction notes. The student says to the teacher: "Do you know what your trouble is? You can't see what you are doing!"

Sensory perception, and interpretation. This is what the process is all about. One of the most important things, then, is our skills of observation. And of course if we are to carve the subject at some time in the future, then our memory becomes the next most important thing.

In this chapter, we will concentrate on developing our observational skills and working out the best way to record what we see for our future reference.

Development of Observational Skills

If you are asked to think of what a horse looks like, you see a certain image in your mind's eye. If you are asked to draw what you see there, chances are you can't. Assuming you have normal hand-eye coordination, then the most likely reason you can't draw what is in your mind's eye is that you really don't know what a horse looks like at all. That is, you have an idea as to the basic parameters of the horse, but when it comes to detail you let yourself down rather badly. Now, this is not because you have a bad memory, it is simply because you didn't put much in there in the first place. And that is because you didn't really take any notice of what you were looking at. You didn't pay attention to

detail. You didn't notice that the horse's eye looks down his nose, or which way his ears are normally facing, or whether his forehead is flat, or what the shape of the cross section of his neck is. It's the same if you were asked to draw an oak leaf. Are the ends of the segments round or pointed? How many are there? Are the veins raised on the front or the back? Are they raised at all? Or your very best friend's face? Could you draw even a vague impression of it? Probably not.

So how are we to go about improving our expertise?

The best way is to discipline ourselves to be considerably more observant in the first place. The next time you look at a leaf, take a few extra moments to look at the curves and twists. The veins and how they are formed. There mightn't even be any veins visible at all. The thickness of the stem. Is the end pointed or like a paddle? Is the surface smooth or rippled?

If perhaps you have been involved as a navigator or a lookout or maybe have had some training as an observer of some kind, your observational discipline will be above average. You will automatically look for things such as shape, shine, shadow, and silhouette. You will have this discipline because you learned to search for detail. So that is what we must do as woodcarvers. That is, if we want to be able to reproduce what we are looking at, we must learn to search for and observe detail.

One way to do this is to start to draw what we are looking at. Simple outlines at first will do. Take a leaf, for example. You could even press it onto the paper and trace around it. Or place the leaf on your drawing paper and trace around its shadow. That is a start. Anything that will begin to force the issue of recording what the detail actually is, and anything that forces you to observe that detail in the first place.

The art of drawing obviously needs practice. Any skill does. So do just that. But before we start, we need to take a few steps backwards, and take some time out to consider what we will need in our kit to do our drawings.

Choosing Drawing Materials

It is important to be clear from the outset that we are not trying to turn ourselves into top-flight drawing artists. It is equally important, however, to understand that we need to create accurate and easy-to-understand records for ourselves. We should select art materials that are easy for us to use and those that will store well.

What to Draw on

A sketchbook with hard covers is ideal—one that can be easily carried around and won't be damaged easily, say, 8½ × 11 in (225 × 280mm) at the largest, and can be used without having to rest on a hard surface like a table that won't be there when you need it. So a firm back cover is essential. This will become your personal woodcarver's idea book. In it record any design idea you come up with—you will be amazed at the number you record over a few months!

Over time, chemically untreated paper may become quite yellow and make it difficult to see your drawings. So, ask and be sure that the paper in your sketch pad has a long life, colorwise (acid-free). The drawings you'll be doing will be for clarity of detail (including written instructions) and not for artistic mood, so the paper needs to be able to reproduce clear, crisp, and clean lines. Don't get paper that is soft or "furry."

What to Draw with

Pencil is best and easiest to use. Avoid ink, as it is too easy to smudge, especially if you are out in the field, and crayon won't generally give you a sufficiently sharp image. You will need to experiment a bit with the degree of hardness or softness to find the one that suits you best. A 4H lead is so hard as to make a line that is too light and difficult to see, and a 6B will be the opposite. HB is generally in the middle. Try different ones, and find your own "comfort zone." Use the harder varieties for detail and the softer varieties for any necessary shading. Whatever you do, remember that the kinds of drawing you will be doing are for the recording of shapes and carving instructions, not for making portraits.

Use a top-quality soft eraser—that is about all you need. Except for a chisel or carver's knife or pencil sharpener to sharpen your pencils (unless you use a mechanical pencil of some sort).

What to Draw?

Draw what you want to carve, of course. But that isn't the real question. We need to be able to work out what we can in fact carve. Then we can get on and draw it and write our instructions.

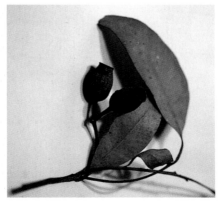

4-1. Unless the components of the leaf, urn, and stem are rearranged, this would be a very difficult subject to carve.

Aside from all the personal choices we might make, there are some things we should take into consideration when we are selecting our carving subjects. Answering the question "What to carve?" is a bit like determining the length of an endless piece of string. The variables are not only tempered as we have already said by our own personal choices, but by our skill level, the wood we have available to us, the time we have at hand, and so on. Given this considerable variation of constraints, the best we can put down for the moment is a range of things to watch out for and to put into our "melting pot."

Consider the following example:

Look at 4-1, which shows a dried sample of the leaf and seed from the native Australian red bloodwood tree, *Eucalyptus gumnifera*. In answer to the question "Can I carve it?" and therefore "Should I draw it?" the following notes could be applied:

You will need to distinguish between the real parts of the object and the background shadows. We will come back to this later.

The stems of the seed urns are very thin, and unless they are attached somehow to a background they will almost certainly break away.

The carving would require the direction of the wood grain to be either along the stems and therefore across the leaf or the reverse, unless the carving were "built" from individual components attached together. Along the leaf and across the stem would be the weakest of the three and the "built" version the strongest.

To hold the carving while in progress would be a virtual impossibility without its completely breaking up.

Overall, this is not a very good subject to carve, unless major modifications are made. If we rearrange the leaf and urn components, however, we can overcome a lot of the challenges listed. Here's what we could do:

Arrange the stems so that they lie in the same direction as the leaf; therefore the wood grain goes along rather than across the stems/leaf. To maintain an "authentic" look, build up the stems from separate pieces, and alter the angle of the stems to the urns and have them going vertically.

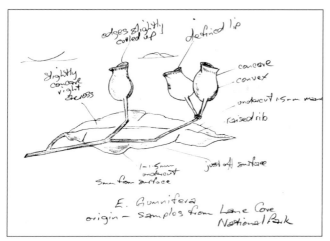

4-2. By rearranging the elements of the sample, we can devise a far more practical layout for carving.

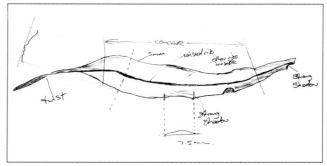

4-3. A separate drawing can be used to show the detail of a particular component more clearly. Once again, there are insufficient measurements to allow accurate reproduction.

Attach the thin stems to the leaf, which would act as the background, helping to protect them from breaking. Attach the urns to the grounding behind the leaf, stabilizing them and helping to stop them from breaking too.

We have taken something that would be exceptionally difficult and made it quite probable, without destroying the realism. The rearrangement is shown in 4-2. The detail of a leaf is shown in 4-3. Note that we have removed all of the shadows that are in the original (refer to 4-1). When you are doing your sketches, it is important wherever possible to have good all-round lighting on the subject so that you pick up the full detail. If you look again at 4-1, it could be a bit difficult to distinguish in places between the real stems and the shadows.

There is nothing of an "artistic" and/or artificial nature about the drawing in 4-2 and 4-3; it is clean and clear, and shows the subject for what it is. It was done with an HB lead mechanical pencil. Another possible arrangement is shown in 4-4.

Once we have realized the limitations of the subject, we can then apply corrective measures, and we are a step closer to making the impossible come true. The application of this principle to any subject we choose will soon open up to us an amazing world of possibilities that we might otherwise discard. And that is just about the most important thing at this stage: to realize that we can probably carve just about anything we can think of—give or take a bit of rearranging.

Nonetheless, there is a huge variety of natural subject matter that is extremely difficult if not impossible to create, no matter what we do. Consider 4-5:

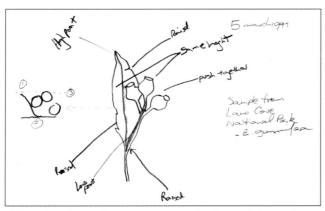

4-4. In this alternative rearrangement the shape of the urn is nothing like the original in 4-1.

4-5. The Queen of the Night would not make an ideal carving subject: tiny, intricate detail does not transfer easily into wood, particularly if good realism is required.

Here is the cactus flower "Queen of the Night" (*Selenicereus grandiflorus*). It flowers only at night, the flower opens once, spreads its perfume into the air, and dies. Spectacular, yes, but as for being a potential carving subject, very problematical. The long, thin petals with their fine tips each moving off in different directions make it basically impossible to carve, unless it is done in the "built-up" manner. Even then the fine tips will tend to break off. And what about the stamens? How to reproduce a mass of them is almost beyond comprehension.

Another serious consideration from the "carvability" point of view is the depth of the flower. To try to carve the center in one piece would be a nightmare at best. Even if built up, the degree of difficulty of shaping the individual pieces would be high. To mount the carving so that it is displayed but protected from damage would be very difficult, unless perhaps it were fully enclosed in a display case, this also being preferable to keeping it from collecting a lot of dust and ultimately being quite off color! This brings us to the additional question "What tools do we have available to us?"

Not only are we limited by our manual skill and the reality of practicality generally, we are also limited by our tool kit. Unless we have unlimited budgets, there is not much point in a carving that will require a substantial purchase of new tools. There will always be new tools we will want to buy—that is the nature of them—but to set out with an objective in mind that requires a substantial outlay may not please us very much in the end, and indeed may make the project frustratingly impossible. The wood that is available is also obviously critical—a soft, fine grain would be ideal, and a hard, coarse grain the opposite.

Storing Nature Samples

At the expense of stating the obvious, if you collect nature samples that are fresh and green and healthy, remember they are going to die. In itself this is no surprise—but it is what happens when they die that you should become familiar with. Wood itself will in most cases shrink, and in some cases crack and split and warp, often depending on the environment in which it is stored.

Flowers will most often discolor significantly, and shrivel and sag into shapeless waste. Grasses and other grain groups will most likely go from green to brown but will probably generally hold their shape, except that

the seeds, if they have any, will probably fall off. An acorn seed will shrink at a different rate than the cup it sits in, and will fall out of it and be quite out of proportion if you put the two back together. Leaves will go brittle and shrink and crinkle, if they don't just sag into an unhappy heap. Certainly you must keep them from dampness, otherwise mold and rot will be the result—remember that there is plenty of water, and most likely mold bacteria, in them in the first place.

All in all, not a happy picture. Unless you can find a way of preserving your specimens, there isn't much choice but to record their details in a model or a drawing. So far, well-documented drawings look to be a pretty attractive proposition for the long term.

Writing Carving Instructions

The reason for the addition to our drawing of instructions for future reference is self-evident, but what is not quite so obvious to us at the time we are doing our drawing is what instructions we should write to ourselves. We are bound to leave out the most important parts—but we won't know what they are until we come to carve it! So, let's look again at 4-2 and see if we can identify what is missing:

> ✳ How big are the leaves and urns? There is no way of knowing. There are no measurements of the subject itself.
> ✳ Are the urns hollow? Presumably, but it doesn't say so.
> ✳ Are the urns round (circular) or elliptical? We don't know.
> ✳ How thick is the urn wall? We don't know.
> ✳ How thick is the leaf? We may not be able to carve it quite as thin as it is in real life, but we don't know how thin that is, anyway.
> ✳ What is the nature of the surface of the urns and leaf? Are they textured in any way? Are they smooth? And the stems? We don't know.

There are two vague cross-section notes (one is in the top left-hand corner), but they are not nearly adequate. In five years' time when we can't remember a thing and there are no red bloodwood trees about anyway, we will never know just what twists and turns the leaf takes along its length. So we have no way of really getting down to a realistic reproduction of the leaf at all.

All in all, we have a nice drawing that is next to useless if we are relying on it for our future woodcarving purposes! We do know where the leaf came from, though (Lane Cove National Park in Sydney, Australia), and we do know when (March 5, 1997), and we have its botanical name. This might just save the day if we want to get more samples. At least we would know when and where we might go to get what.

It is imperative, therefore, that we take a great deal more care to record much further detail than is in the drawing shown in 4-2. It really tells us not much at all, and if we do rely on it for a carving in the future, we could be quite disappointed with the result of our labors.

So, what we will do is move on and make our reference model, and then come back and take another look at our drawing.

Making a Reference Model

Which Medium to Use for Modeling?
There are a great variety of modeling media, however, the most common being natural wet clay, plaster, Plasticine, and wax. Each has its own general characteristics, each is good for particular things, and each comes in a range of specifications to suit a purpose. It is important to try as many different media as possible, so that you can find your own comfort zone and the one that best suits your circumstance and needs.

About Wet Natural Clay
Naturally occurring clay is available in different colors and grades, and can be stored in dry powder form or moistened with water. Natural clay is fairly inexpensive, and can be reworked before it is "fired." Unless it is fired, it may well remain brittle and crumble easily when it dries, if it is not stored in a very safe place. It may also shrink and crack, and for this reason it must be kept damp with a regular spraying of water (from an atomizer, for example) and kept wrapped in a damp cloth while it is being worked. A fine grade of clay is best for most applications, and it is easily shaped with simple wooden knives that you can make yourself.

About Plaster
"Plaster of Paris" is prepared commercially from calcium sulfate, and is a dry powder that easily mixes with water to form a thick cream. When subsequently dried, it forms a solid mass that no longer reacts with water.

Once set to the right consistency, plaster can easily be shaped with the same knives that you used for clay. It can also be shaped to a certain extent after it has completely hardened, although it can be brittle and powdery. It needs to be mixed thoroughly, as it can easily get either lumpy, in which case it will not form a uniform solid mass, or filled with air bubbles, which will definitely end up in the wrong place and give you holes where you don't want them!

Plaster can also be brittle and easily break and crumble if not stored securely.

About Plasticine
Plasticine is available in different colors and densities, and reacts with heat to go soft and pliable. This can be its greatest downside, inasmuch as it can easily move on a hot day unless it is stabilized with an "armature" (an internal supporting structure such as wire). It is very easily shaped with the fingers and modeling knives, as most of us remember from our school days. Use one of the harder varieties, so that you can get better detail, and you are less likely to lose the shape on a warm day. Whatever you do, don't store Plasticine near a source of heat, especially after you have spent hours shaping it.

About Wax
This is an excellent medium to try. Wax, like Plasticine, is heat-sensitive; however, there is a range of waxes with different melting points, some of them reasonably high, so that provided the thickness of the wax is sufficient, even on a hot day (85 degrees F or 30 degrees C) there will be no loss of form. Some of the best kinds are petroleum derivatives, and they are specially manufactured for sculpting purposes.

It is important that they be heated through very evenly, otherwise they, too, can go lumpy and crumble at the wrong time. The heat sensitivity is so good in some of these products that body warmth from your hands is very quickly transferred to the wax—and this is one of wax's other outstanding features—the speed with which it goes hot and cold, making it stable and good to work with.

When cold and quite hard, modeling waxes can also be carved with knives and your old chisels. Wax can also be continuously recycled, making it economical from this point of view, although of all the modeling media it is probably the most expensive to buy.

A fine surface finish can be achieved with petroleum-derivative waxes by first smoothing them thoroughly with a flat metal blade such as the end of a skew chisel, and then hand rubbing with paraffin oil.

If you are sculpting a large hollow object such as a bust, then perfect stability can be achieved by filling the hollow wax with an aerosol foam, which also avoids having to have a solid core of wax, which would make the sculpture very heavy. We will use wax to make a model from our eucalyptus leaf drawing.

Making the Model

To begin modeling it is first necessary to set up a firm base. In this exercise, an offcut of ⅜ in (10mm) ply was coated with a ⅛-in (3mm) layer of wax to establish a working surface (see 4-6).

The leaf is next, and a piece of wax slightly less than ⅛ in (3mm) thick was made by rolling a lump warmed in the hand. The wax takes up body heat quickly, and can be rolled with a short length of ½-in (13mm) dowel used like a rolling pin. A few drops of paraffin oil will keep it lubricated and stop it from sticking to the dowel.

4-6. Wax makes an excellent modeling medium. Good detail can be achieved and it is stable and easy to store.

The thin layer of wax, cut to the approximate shape with a knife, is laid on the background, and the contours of the cross section bent into the leaf before it is finally adhered. Melting the surface of the background layer and/or the back of the leaf with a lighted match (whichever you find easiest) does this. Just a few seconds' exposure to the flame is sufficient.

The thin "rib" down the center of the leaf is made by rolling a small piece of wax between your fingers. It might break a couple of times before you are successful; however, it will be good practice for making the stems for the urns.

Joining the stems for the urns is done similarly, by melting the ends of the wax "sticks" with a match. The wax will melt very quickly and form little knobs at the join, which coincidentally is fairly realistic for this species. In our example, the urns, fashioned in the fingers, and with the help of a knife, are rolled in sawdust to give a textural difference, increasing the "natural" look. The live leaf is smoother and before it dries out is shinier than the urns.

During this modeling activity, if this is the first time you have ever tried it, you will make some interesting discoveries about the way in which your hands interpret what your eyes see—or don't see, as the case may be! Examples of various first efforts at modeling are shown in 4-7, 4-8, 4-9, and 4-10.

4-7. The stems of the urns should be straight, not bent.

4-8. The stems are too thick, and they should not be tapered like mouse tails.

Remember, in every case, we are talking about the transfer of what we observe into the modeled form. So, if our observation is incorrect in the first place, it will be impossible to build a correct likeness. In 4-7, the really obvious error is that the stems are curving out of their junctions, rather than coming out straight. So we have bent stems rather than straight ones. The stems on the right are not as "bad" as on the left. This model is from wax.

The model seen in 4-8 is from Plasticine. Notice that the surface is more "oily"-looking than wax. The urns are more like mice on the run! The shape of the urns isn't all bad; however, the stems are too thick and are not as straight as they should be.

In the model seen in 4-9, the urns have flat bottoms rather than round ones, and the opening at the tops of the urns is not as "lipped" as it should be. The modeling tool in the diagram is an old dentist's tamper—these sorts of dentist's tools are excellent for modeling. Unfortunately, the incorrect "geometry" of the model is very noticeable. Why would the urn have a flat bottom?

A sphere that isn't, a straight line that's crooked, and urns that are square are all very visible errors, because they are the most predominant shapes of the whole object. They in fact form basic characteristics that are the most memorable features of the nuts. It is very important, therefore, to get these shapes right.

The model shown in 4-10 is from clay. The basic shapes are reasonably well rendered, the leaf taking on the sometimes characteristic "crinkly" look of the eucalyptus leaf as it dries out. What we have done, however, is to make the "ribs" quite incorrectly. They look nothing like this in 4-1.

4-9. Flat bottoms are definitely not a characteristic of the red bloodwood urn.

4-10. The ribs in this leaf are the opposite of what they should be.

It is the detail that is letting us down here. The ribs are in fact raised up, not set in, and the center rib is very prominent, the radial ribs being very faint. Reality is quite the opposite of this clay model.

Our observational skills, therefore, need some refinement before we can expect to achieve a correct rendition of the leaf. Another detail missing from 4-10 is that the stems are not in the model. Note the characteristic "lanky" stems in 4-1? They are not reproduced at all. Thus, we again lose one of the important characteristics that make the species recognizable.

At least, though, the "form work" is much better in this example. It is only the "decoration" that is basically wrong. And that is not a bad way to look at the steps in producing your model. Get the form right first, then decorate it. We will use this phrase throughout our learning process. Form first, decorate later!

Recording Measurements

We have said a lot about what is wrong with our drawing, so as we have the finished model, we could now work "backwards" and add what is missing to our drawing. The two most important things are the scale of the drawing and sufficient cross-section information to make a reasonably authentic shape, especially for the leaf.

The easiest way to do the sizing is to do the original drawing actual size, and note this on it, together with some key measurements like length and width. Scale is obviously needed if the page size isn't big enough. When choosing a scale, make things easy for yourself and select one that is easy to translate into actual size—a multiple of two or three, for example, so you can do the calculations quickly in your head.

If each part of the drawing is correct in relation to size, then it should be necessary to record the measurements of only one or two of the parts. Whichever method you choose, be sure that you are consistent in its use throughout your drawing.

Recording Cross Sections

Recording cross sections is vital if we are to reproduce a realistic model. Unfortunately, they are not so easy to work out.

The leaf shape in 4-11, carved from American walnut, was cut laterally through the middle of the curled edge, to produce the cross section shown in 4-12. It is these sorts of cross section that you will need to draw. Accurate drawing of cross sections will certainly develop your skills of observation.

The more cross sections we do in our drawings the better, up to a point—after which it is counterproductive to keep doing them. The important thing is to draw cross sections at least where there are significant alterations to shape or direction. Generally it will be reasonably easy to work out the "fill-in shape" between these sections when you commence carving.

4-11. To accurately record the surface contours of the subject, it may be necessary to cut through it. If this is not practical, careful study will be required.

4-12. This is the cross section of 4-11 cut laterally through the middle.

An Example of Professional Drawings

Every professional woodcarver will do drawings and write instructions, and normally they will be kept filed for future reference. Occasionally historical records are presented to museums, and if a museum near you has such a set of professional drawings in its archives, it is well worth arranging for a viewing. Such a set exists in the Powerhouse Museum in Sydney, Australia. The archival collection was the property of a Mr. Frederick William Tod, (Dec. 1879–June 1958). Tod migrated from England to Sydney in 1915, where he quickly became a well-known and highly respected woodcarver; many examples of his fine work remain throughout New South Wales.

4-13. On the left is a computer-generated enhancement of a drawing done by woodcarver Frederick Tod for the eagle lectern for St. John's Church in Gordon, Sydney, Australia, and shown in 4-16. On the right is another computer-generated enhancement of a drawing Tod did for his design and positioning for the eagle's feet.

The original drawings are held in the Powerhouse Museum, in Sydney, and were done on a roll of brown paper, in pencil and crayon. The drawing is now very hard to see, as the paper is quite yellow and the pencil faded. Compare the drawings to the actual lectern and you will see how faithful the carving is to the original concept.

4-14. The head of the carved eagle is slightly more elevated and less fearful than the drawing, and the wings are also higher.

4-15. The positioning of the feet very closely follows the drawing.

4-16. Frederick Tod's Eagle Lectern, circa 1930.

The collection of drawings in the Powerhouse Museum includes one of an eagle lectern, which is in use at the local Sydney church of St. John in Gordon. We can see in 4-13 computer-enhanced graphics of a photograph of the original drawings, which are rapidly fading as a pencil and crayon sketch on a brown paper scroll. The intended shape and positioning of the eagle's feet are seen on the right on 4-13 as they were to appear on the sphere atop the lectern's pedestal.

Fortunately, included with the drawing are some instructions that Frederick Tod wrote as a guide to the construction of the bird. They are obviously intended as a guide to carpenters dressing the wood for carving, and the numbers are presumably measurements in Imperial inches. The inscription is as follows:

"As 5 × 5 only finishes 4½ and only 1½ for wings and back available finishing at ⅜ an additional ⅞ must be stuck on back of bird square central line at body of bird before starting carving and bore holes first reverse this [pattern] to bore holes in body of bird . . ."

The results of the drawing and its instructions are shown in 4-14, 4-15, and 4-16. The date of completion of the lectern is not known, although it would be in the vicinity of 1920–1930.

Finally, part of a picture frame also by Tod is seen in 4-17. It was never assembled. The carving is in maple, and is of the same red bloodwood species as the very first of the sample urn and leaves at the beginning of this chapter. The urns are not open in this carving, and the central one in the cluster of three in the middle of the carving is "in flower."

4-17. Australian red bloodwood leaves and flowers, Frederick Tod, circa 1940.

chapter 5

YOU CAN START CARVING NOW!

Your Opening Moves

To say most people are "frightened" to make their first chisel cuts is most likely an understatement. This chapter takes you through the fear barrier. You will come out the other side less timid, less rigid, and less frightened of making a mistake. You will realize that, as with most art forms, if you make what you think is a mistake, you can almost (though not always) fix it without anyone realizing you went wrong in the first place. However, this chapter isn't about the "cover-up"—it is about getting to know your basic tools, how they work, and what they do.

The four exercises I discuss in this chapter are deliberately chosen and placed in a particular sequence to help you develop your skills. This chapter is also very important from the point of view of the development of an understanding of the use of shadows. Each example is designed to build on the skills developed in the preceding example, and it would be unfair to yourself to tackle the fourth one before you've done the first three in the right order.

The woods chosen for these exercises have also been selected for specific reasons. Each has a totally different grain characteristic and density, and each one behaves quite differently under the same tool. If you do the four exercises, it is important that you try different woods for each, so that you start to build experiences with different woods in different situations. If you can't obtain the actual woods used, some alternatives are listed with each exercise.

Three Teardrops

Our first exercise is a simple three-teardrop design (see 5-1). The design is not a thing of great beauty, but rather it is an exercise chosen to develop skills in using the skew chisel correctly. The skew is the most versatile of all the tool shapes, yet it is the simplest. Unfortunately for some of us it is also one of the most difficult to master, because it requires development of the use of the fingers and hand to operate the tool in a paring and slicing action, rather than straight "digging" or "pushing." A skew anywhere between ³⁄₁₆ and ¾ in (4 and 20mm) wide is ideal for this exercise. Try a smaller size first; however, you may also find a larger one easier to manage. Because of the degree of difficulty in using this tool, we will start with a design that substantially requires its use. If you can master the skew, then you can master any of the other tools with great ease. Using the skew helps you to understand the challenges of grain direction, which aren't quite so obvious when starting out with a regular gouge.

To set up this carving, first transfer the pattern to your wood, and then cut around the perimeter with a scroll saw or coping saw. Mount it on a backboard with paper in between and clamp it firmly to your bench. Use a soft wood like meranti (on the right of 5-2) or linden/lime (on the left of 5-2), dressed to ½ in (13mm). Make your pattern 3 in (75mm) wide (from the apex to the end of the largest teardrop).

Then, with your skew, cut around each teardrop with a vertical incision, going about ⅛ in (3mm) deep to start. Cut away the waste wood around each drop, progres-

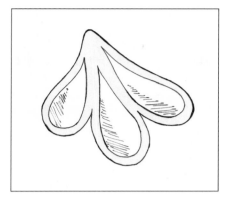

5-1. Your three teardrops for exercise one. See Chapter 2 for discussions of pattern transferring and holding devices. This piece is glued to a backboard with a piece of paper between.

sively going deeper until you are about halfway through the piece of wood. In the maple example in 5-2, the left teardrop has been cut to halfway, with a flat background created around it; the shaping of the drop has been started in the central teardrop, and the one on the right is basically completed. Use a ¼-in (6mm) almost flat gouge for leveling the background, or try using a small skew.

If you can complete this design with nothing other than a skew chisel, you are doing particularly well from a "beginner's" point of view. You may well need just a relatively flat ³⁄₁₆-in (4mm) straight gouge to clean up the background; however, it could be done with a small skew. Your skew can also be used very effectively as a scraper for cleaning up a "furry" surface.

As with all the chisels that you'll be using, it's very important that when you are finding your own comfort zone you make sure you consider the aspect of tool control. When we're carving, some of us find that the closer our hands are to the sharp end of the chisel, the greater control we have. So we do not tend to hold the tool by the handle at all because the hand is too far away from the end of the tool, and the chisel tends to wobble all over the place. We hold the chisel right down low, as close to the cutting edge as possible. You may well find that this practice works for you, too. Refer to Chapter 2.

5-2. Linden (lime) or meranti is suitable wood to start with. See if you can complete the entire exercise with a skew.

What you will discover about your skew is the difficulty in actually holding it and getting it to do anything. In effect you can use the tool any way you wish in terms of pushing, pulling, or paring. It is a matter of finding your own comfort zone—there are no rules, except that if you find what works for you, then do it. It is the result that matters, not how you get there.

A major part of the establishment of your personal comfort is to try both left- and right-handed activity. While your brain is "scrambled," trying to understand its new activity, is the best time to experiment with being ambidextrous. For a woodcarver to be ambidextrous is a great advantage. If your work is on a bench that is up against a wall, and you are working on it right-handed and need to approach it from the other direction, it is a significant nuisance to have to unclamp it and turn it around all the time. This we discussed in Chapter 2. You will find that an ability to readily swap hands without interrupting your workflow is extremely useful. Normally, a right-handed carver would hold the chisel in the left hand and the mallet in the right. Interestingly, some of us who are right-handed suddenly find that we are better at left-handed carving!

You will also find from now on just how important the angle of the bevel is with regard to the ease of use of the tool. You'll recall from Chapter 2 the discussion on how the angle of the bevel dictates the behavior of the chisel. You will find with the skew chisel, in particular, that if the degree of curve on the bevel is unsuitable for the way you want to hold it in the wood you are working with, you will have extreme difficulty in getting it to cut at all. So what we do need to do now is start experimenting with the shape of this bevel to get it to suit not only the wood, but also the way we hold the tool.

If the bevel on your skew is too convex, you are going to find that it is too difficult to get a cutting action going without holding the chisel extremely vertically. If the bevel is, on the other hand, too flat, or indeed "hollow ground," you are going to find that

5-3. Cutting in the direction of the arrow to the left produces a smoother cut than that of the arrow to the right, where the skew digs into the grain.

you are forever digging the chisel in and making a mess of the surface. You need to find the balance, or the equilibrium, between the way you hold the tool and the medium that you're working in. If you find the skew slips off the surface without cutting, either it is blunt or the convex curve on the bevel is too great, or both. First, sharpen it, then retest, and if it still happens, flatten out the bevel until you get it working for you.

If this is the first time you have held a carving tool, you may find your nervousness or timidity in approaching the wood becomes an impediment to good results. This is perfectly normal. You may be nervous enough to be holding the tool too tightly, so you are strangling it—your knuckles will go white, and you'll get sore fingers. You'll find that you're so tense that you're hardly doing any cutting at all, just picking at the wood. You'll be picking and poking, rather than slicing and shaving.

As a result of this picking and poking you'll find that there will be a very rough surface in the end and you'll have digs all over the place. You'll be going against the grain, against the fibers, the wood will chip and split, and you'll probably end up with largely a mess, like 5-3. Don't let these things cause you despair—they are all perfectly normal.

What you need to do is to relax, take your time, consider each move carefully, and don't be worried about making a mistake. Don't forget it is only a piece of wood, and you can always start again.

It is very important that you understand the direction of the grain and its relativity to the curve that you are trying to cut along. You'll find very quickly that the wood will tell you what it wants you to do to it. If it doesn't like what you do to it, it'll split and crack, but if it does like what you are doing it'll cut with a nice smooth surface. The results are quite visibly obvious. You'll certainly be able to feel the different responses of the wood, the tool flowing through the wood in the right direction and grating and jarring in the wrong direction.

5-4. If you get your first carving to look like this, stop and move to the next one. Come back later and have a go at tidying it up.

There are a number of things to observe in 5-4. First, the surfaces of the teardrops have been smoothed over with abrasive paper, but not very perfectly. See the facets on the edges? They are still there, made duller by the paper, but there nonetheless. The standard of finish you achieve will be a very important part of the carving process. If your work doesn't look any good when you have finished, all the hours you put into it will have been for nothing. So, if you are going to sand it, sand it completely. Next, the surface texture of the drops is different from the background. This is because the sanding was not done on the background. It is important to be aware that sanding changes texture and this can alter the light reflection from the surface and even make the wood have different color intensity.

The rough background is there because the tool used to smooth it wasn't sharp enough. Also, there are some cuts in the background, just to the right of the central drop. These are there because the vertical incisions that were made were too deep or, alternatively, the background wasn't taken deep enough. It will be important to learn to accurately estimate the depth of these vertical cuts, which are also called stop-cuts.

5-5. For this exercise you could use jelutong, devil tree (cheese-wood), linden (lime), or basswood or similar softer woods.

Now, if this is your first carving, and you can get it to the standard in 5-4, the best advice for you is to stop working on it and move on to the next exercise. This is not to encourage incomplete work, but rather to ensure that you do not enter a period of frustration or even boredom that will clearly be counterproductive. It is vital that you move forward all the time, returning to this carving if you wish to at a later time to tidy it up, using new skills that you have learned and new tools that you want to experiment with. Remember our cry: Experiment, experiment, experiment!

Renaissance-Style Leaf

This is the kind of pattern that might be added to a piece of furniture such as a bed headboard or cupboard door. This exercise will again require the use of the skew chisel, and we will add a gouge and V-tool. In this exercise, pay particular attention to the flowing curves and the need to execute visually pleasing shapes. Aesthetics, for the first time, start to become an issue. The teardrop pattern has a limited capacity to appeal to the eye, although it is reasonable if well executed. This second pattern, however, introduces us to flowing moving lines, layers, different depths, and the real use of shadows.

The pattern in 5-5 is traced using carbon paper on jelutong prepared to a thickness of 1 in (25mm), breadth 3 in (75mm), and length 7 in (180mm), the grain running longitudinally. The pattern is then cut out with the scroll saw and glued with a cardboard "sandwich" to the backboard (see 5-6).

5-6. A light-colored wood is used for this exercise so that the ridgeline you will carve into it is very clearly visible with cross lighting. See Chapter 1, "About Light."

5-7. *Vital to the success of this carving is the clean sweep of the ridgeline, which becomes very clearly visible with strong cross lighting.*

5-8. *In different lighting conditions, you see quite different things. It is important to have movable lighting at your workbench.*

With this exercise, the easiest way to get a pleasing, flowing "sweep" to the curves is to use the same gouge for all the carving along its length. Select a gouge for the concave curve that you will use for the entirety of that curve. Use the skew for the convex curves. Until we have developed our skills further, we don't want to start doing the concave curve with one gouge and halfway through the curve use a different shape. We run the risk at this stage of our development of getting an untidy junction where the two gouge cuts meet.

You'll notice once again that lighting is extremely important. Note that one of the key focal points (more accurately "focal lines") in this design is the ridge that runs along the center of the leaf. Both focal points and lines will become very important to us as we progress through the next chapters. If this ridge is not a pleasing, even curve, it will be very obvious to the eye that it isn't, and it will have a very displeasing effect on the viewer. It's a bit similar to a straight line that's crooked or a circle that isn't round.

One of the most important parts of this carving, then, is to get a continuous, uninterrupted, even sweep (curve) along the focal line. The top half of the leaf, the part not in shadow in 5-7, is a compound curve of both convex and concave shapes. The leaf segment second from the right is convex, and the last segment (the long one) is convex at the base of the third-from-the-right segment. We will use the same gouge we used for the concave curve that is in the shadow to complete all the concave curves, and we'll

use the skew chisel once again to create the convex curves. A good gouge shape for this carving is a ¾-in (20mm) wide, relatively shallow curve, shown in the side boxes in Chapter 2, "Which Tool?"

You'll note also that the different parts of the leaf above and below the ridgeline are at different levels, or layers. This adds to the ability of the carving to make an interesting set of shadows. There are two convex curves, and while they are subtle, they make a considerable difference in the overall "look" of the pattern. You'll notice also in the overall pattern that the long sweep of the ridge starts high from the background on the right hand end, where the stalk of the leaf might be, and slopes gradually down to its tip. So throughout this carving, we have compound curves from one end to the other, and from top half to bottom half, creating quite interesting shadow effects, albeit with a fairly simple design. As we have said, when you think relief, think shadow. The view in 5-8 is lit with a duller light at a different angle. What you can see is quite different from 5-7. Notice the facets on the second leaf segment from the top right—this is supposed to be convex!

Jelutong—a very soft wood primarily from Malaysia that may be difficult to obtain in parts of North America—is a very unforgiving wood, particularly with blunt tools. If your tools aren't beautifully sharp, you'll get tearing on the surface. You will be able to hear it and see it and feel it, in precisely the same way you did in the side boxes in Chapter 2 "Which Tool?" and you'll certainly be able to see all the bad lines because the shadows will be very strong. We will need to ensure that the concave curves are cut cleanly with the gouge and the convex curves are cut smoothly with the skew. There will be no room for blunt tools or sloppy workmanship.

Equally important are the small veins put in with the V-tool. You can see them in 5-7. These shadows simply decorate the surface. Don't overdo them, because there isn't a great amount of room, and don't make them too deep, otherwise they will look like unfortunate scars. If they are too long they will look out of balance; and don't put too many of them on either, otherwise they'll look rather silly. So you can see there is a lot to think about with such a simple decoration!

If you find that the surface of the jelutong along the sharp edges of the leaf is chipping, you actually need to blunt that edge of the wood by chamfering it off so that it doesn't continue to fracture. You will also find that the sharper the tool, the cleaner the cut, and therefore the less likelihood of fracturing's taking place. In this exercise not only is the creation of pleasing shadows of extreme importance, but the use of very sharp tools to get there is equally so.

If your tools are sharp and your hand steady, it will be unnecessary to use abrasive paper to "clean up." Because jelutong is so soft, paper changes its surface texture and shape dramatically, so be careful if you do use it.

As you work the jelutong with the gouge, you will find very quickly that cutting against the grain creates a rough-split surface. Cutting with the grain is quite satisfactory, and after a bit of experimentation you'll also discover that diagonally across and with the grain is perhaps the best direction to move your tool. You'll get the cleanest cut without breaking the surface fibers. The best thing to do, though, is to experiment, and you will very soon be able to find the best direction to approach the lay of the grain.

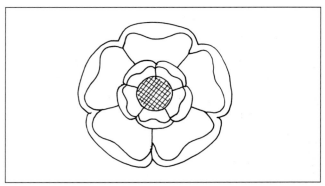

5-9. *Trace the rose from the drawing, enlarge it to 3 in (75mm) across, and transfer it to the wood in the normal manner. Use white carbon or white pencil for darker woods.*

Tudor Rose

The detail seen in 5-9 is of a Tudor-style rose taken from the misericord in Chester Cathedral in England, seen in 5-10. The primary objective of this exercise is to introduce you to the interpretation of photographs of woodcarvings and to introduce you to additional basic tools that you'll use for the remainder of your carving career. The wood chosen for this exercise is black bean. It is a Queensland (Australia) subtropical species and was commonly used in Australia for the manufacture of church pews and decorative ecclesiastical carvings. You could also use American walnut or European oak.

5-10. *This misericord is in Chester Cathedral in England. The flower pattern is known as a "Tudor rose."*

Note that the sanding dust and sawdust from black bean is highly toxic and may very quickly affect your mucous membranes throughout your nose, throat, and chest, so if you do use this wood, it is advised you use a respirator when sanding or sawing.

This exercise requires you to make a representation of the Tudor rose approximately 3 in (75mm) in diameter and approximately 5/16 in (8mm) in overall depth, measuring from the center of the bead in the center of the rose to the background.

Trace the Tudor rose from the illustration, and enlarge it or redraw it to 3 in (75mm) diameter. It is worth noting that in many instances of this kind of historical carving, the patterns are not necessarily symmetrical. Symmetry sometimes equates with an artificial look, particularly with nature subjects, where symmetry rarely exists. When the original carvings were done of this nature they were not symmetrical, they were hand drawn, hand carved, and were representations of design ideas. They were certainly not meant to be a perfect geometry. Hence we have chosen the distorted rose to the left of 5-9 to make it a little more interesting.

Once you've completed your sketch, transfer it onto the wood using carbon paper. "Old-fashioned" blue typist's carbon paper is the most common (although becoming increasingly more difficult to obtain); however, see if you can track down white carbon paper—it is excellent for transferring patterns to darker wood.

Step One—Removing the Background

The first part of the exercise is to "set in" the pattern or "rough out" the background. Do this using the ¾-in (20mm) standard gouge together with your mallet. When you make a vertical cut with your gouge around the pattern, it is called a stop-cut. You make it with the bevel pointing towards the pattern, and you will see the scallops around the edge in 5-11. When you do the clearing cut, with the bevel resting where the background will be, and you are pushing the gouge towards the stop-cut, you run a risk of cutting into the side of the rose and ultimately damaging it.

For this reason, when you make the stop-cuts, hold the gouge with the shaft vertical, and the bevel will push the tool outwards away from the edge, making in fact a sloping edge. Your clearing cuts will then damage only the sloping edge that you must remove later

to make a vertical edge. To make a vertical edge, you will need to hold the bevel vertically, and this will mean that the shaft of the gouge will be leaning outwards from the carving (towards you). The vertical edge can then be undercut to make a strong shadow. (Refer to the discussion on shadows in Chapter 1 and 1-4, 1-5, and 1-6.)

An alternative way to start the setting in process is to take a V-tool and draw around the outside of the pattern with it, to a depth of approximately 1/16 in (2mm). This will help you to see the pattern, and you can also use this groove as a guide for the gouge when you make your stop-cuts. It may also help to stop surface chipping around the top edge of the pattern. You can clean off the shoulders of the scallops that you make with the same gouge, and if it is not too curvy, you can use it to level the background; otherwise, use an almost flat gouge.

You'll notice that your mallet is used in this exercise for both power and control, control being the more important of the two. If you don't hit the tool, it will not move. It is very important that you get used to using your mallet for this purpose. (Refer to Chapter 2, "Which Tool?") Using your mallet for control and power, remove the background so that the center of the bead is about 5/16 in (8mm) above it.

Once the background is removed it's then time to start the actual modeling process. You will need for this exercise at least a ¾-in (20mm) relatively flat gouge, a 6mm slightly curved gouge, a 5/16-in (8mm) V-tool, and a skew chisel.

5-11. Roughing out the pattern uses a combination of stop-cuts and clearing cuts.

Here are some things to observe about the Tudor rose pattern in 5-9 on page 71:

✳ It is not symmetrical.
✳ The length of the spear points is almost the full length of the petal.
✳ There is a rise around the bead that the crosshatch goes over, so you've got the bead in the center and you have the rise between the bead and the petal itself.

Look at the shadows across 5-9, the most obvious ones being the crosshatch, but also note the shadows around the perimeter of the petals themselves, both the inside and the outside. It's important that you recreate these when doing your carving.

Step Two—Setting in the Bead

The second step, then, is to draw in the bead with a compass or freehand. Then, set in the bead using your skew chisel and your ³⁄₁₆ in (4mm) flat gouge. Make a stop-cut (a vertical incision) with the gouge, and with your skew cut in the round sloping edges of the bead and the rise so that you create a trough between them (see 5-12).

Step Three—Create the Petals

Next, hollow out the petals themselves (see 5-12). This is done with your ¼-in (6mm) gouge and your ½-in (13mm) gouge. Then, with your skew, round off the border of the petals. Note the top surface is not round in cross section, but remains rather "flattish." Then cut in the spears with your skew. It is important that you get the edges of the spears flat, and that you create a neat, sharp ridgeline down their center.

Step Four—Cleanup

Once you have each of the elements in place, the next step is to clean up the entire work (see 5-13). Undercut around the inside and the outside of the perimeter of the petals. You will notice as you progress that black bean reacts very favorably to a sharp chisel. Of course every wood will do this; however, in the case of black bean you will find a sharp chisel creates a shiny, waxy surface finish. Black bean naturally has a high wax content, and a blunt chisel tears the fibers and doesn't allow the waxy nature of the wood to be seen in its truest form. A highly polished sharp tool will create a beautiful smooth surface and allow the natural waxy content to be clearly visible. This is the best test for chisel compatibility with black bean.

As you progress with this carving you'll discover that you'll need greater patience than with the first two examples. The wood itself is brittle and wants to fracture and split, the fibers come away very easily, and the only way to combat this and get the desired result is to take your time with very sharp tools. Black bean is not the kind of wood you can hurry with. Mind you, one shouldn't hurry with any wood! You certainly need to take time to keep your chisels really sharp so you'll be constantly using your strop. From this moment on, for woodcarving, patience will be one of your greatest allies.

5-12. Don't forget to leave in the rise between the bead and the entrance to each petal.

5-13. Spend time ensuring that the carving is clean and tidy, before adding the final touches.

The previous examples were both soft woods, certainly significantly softer than black bean, so that a slightly flatter bevel would have been quite advantageous. In the case of black bean, which wants to flake and break, you may find that a very slightly rounder bevel will improve the performance of the chisel in the wood. You may want to experiment in this regard. If you do, remember that it is only a very marginal shift in the angle of the bevel that will make a major shift in the behavior of the tool. You don't have to make significant alterations to the tool to improve (or destroy) its performance under these circumstances. Black walnut and European oak are not as waxy as black bean, but they will behave in a similar way. Walnut has a high silica content and will blunt your tools quickly.

You'll find that the sharpness of your V-tool is critical to the performance of the tool in black bean, and the last thing you want to do is do your crosshatches and have the edges chip and break away. Once you've got a nice neat and tidy surface finish over the entire Tudor rose, make sure that before you put in the crosshatch you ensure that your V-tool is extremely finely polished. Test it on a scrap of black bean or on the back of the piece of wood that you are carving. Make sure it is working properly, otherwise you are tempting fate. The completed rose is seen in 5-14.

5-14. Test that your V-tool is sharp enough before attempting the crosshatch decoration.

The Bishop's Leaf

The Bishop's leaf comes from the throne in St. Andrew's Cathedral, Inverness, Scotland. The back of the Bishop's throne is shown in 5-15.

For this exercise we will use American white oak prepared to a thickness of 1 in (25mm), 5 in (125mm) wide, and 8 in (200mm) long. The carving of this leaf is very much an exercise in the separation of the elements, the setting-in of background, the molding of curves, and, of course, the creation of shadows. Oak is typical for this kind of work; however, American white oak is not a particularly easy variety of oak to carve. It is far more difficult than European or Japanese oak, for instance. The wood is stringy, it tends to chip and flake, and it is not easy for the carver to get a smooth surface—although the carving can be scraped smooth with a very fine, sharp knife.

The order of proceeding for this carving is shown in 5-16 through 5-22. For this carving you will need a ¼-in (6mm) "fluter" (round, deep gouge) in addition to the tools you have already used. If you analyze the leaf shown in 5-21 and 5-22, you will see it has three parts:

❊ the background,
❊ the three segments of the leaf, and
❊ the stem.

Look at the design carefully and you will see that the three parts of the leaf are in fact linked together by a continuous curve. This goes from the outside of the left-hand segment curving around via the stalk and then straight up the middle, creating the first part of the trough that we will cut out. It then curves back around to form the right-hand segment of the leaf. It is a very clever design from this point of view, very simple and very effective. So the center trough separates the two halves of the leaf, which are designated by the stalk in the center. Once the top segment of the leaf is completed, then either one of the left- or right-hand segments of the leaf can be started.

For this carving we will use a two-part template, shown in 5-16, the larger being the major profile, the smaller part being the leaf design that sits over the background. Here is the order of proceeding:

Set in the background as in 5-17. We have chosen a depth of ⅝ in (15mm) so that we have a residual background ⅜ in (10mm) thick. The three-part leaf and its stalk or stem are first set in, being very careful to ensure that the stem of the leaf is not removed accidentally.

5-15. The back of the Bishop's throne, St. Andrew's Cathedral, Inverness, Scotland.

5-16. The large holes drilled in the templates are to hang it on the workshop wall and the three smaller holes locate the templates together, using a small nail. Make a light impression with the points in the wood to be carved in order to line them up perfectly.

5-17. Remove the background to expose the leaf pattern.

5-18. Dig out the central trough.

5-19. Mold the leaves.

Draw in the ridgeline of the stem down from the center of the leaf to the top of the background. This you can clearly see in 5-20 and 5-21. Once the leaf is profiled with the vertical edge all the way around, then we can commence the actual molding of the shape and the creation of the shadows.

The majority of the work will require the skew chisel for the center segment, as it is basically a convex curve. The two lobes—the left and the right parts of the leaf—are a combination of skew work for the convex curves and gouge for the concave portions. It is very important to ensure that the treatment of the stem or stalk of the leaf is carefully thought through. It is an integral part of the design, and the leaf will certainly look very peculiar if the stalk is not positioned and shaped correctly.

In 5-20, 5-21, and 5-22 there is a little curl in the edge of the leaf on the right-hand lobe. The trick is to introduce it so that it makes a lively little shadow to break up an otherwise smooth surface. The little curl that you put on is very much a decoration to the surface of the leaf proper. The use of these decorations is, in design terms, what makes the difference between a good carving and an average one. All the time we are looking for little tricks like this, to enhance an otherwise potentially plain design.

Strong shadows are created underneath this leaf by very severe undercutting, seen clearly in 5-22. You could undercut $\frac{5}{16}$ to $\frac{3}{8}$ in (8 to 10mm) for good effect. What you will find difficult, though, is cleaning up the surface underneath the leaf. The undercut is quite difficult to access, and something you might consider using to clean out the chips and loose fibers is a blunt instrument such as the end of a metal knitting needle. It is quite useful for compressing the fibers back into their place and making a nice, tidy, clean sur-

5-20. Decorate the background.

5-21. Clean up the surface to finish with sealer and wax.

face inside the undercut. You need to be careful, of course, not to score the surface and end up with a line "drawn" by the blunt tool you use.

The details seen in 5-21 clearly show the effectiveness of the decoration of the ribs on the right and the left lobes. If you compare 5-20 without the ribs to 5-21 with, you will see that the use of these ribs creates shadow lines that break up the pattern and once again enhance it together with the curl on the edge on the leaf.

It is important with these sorts of decorations that they are not overdone. The ribs, for example, could be easily too deeply incised, they could be too wide, or they could be too strong in terms of shadow. So you'll need to find a reasonable balance, such that the decoration you are putting on the basic leaf doesn't overwhelm the design and make it look untidy or complicated.

You will notice as you are working this design in this wood that the wood will show every facet you put on it. It's a very hard wood, compared to the ones that we have worked so far; however, with a very sharp chisel you will nevertheless get a polished surface automatically. The wood is also quite absorbent of dirt and dust and will show the grime from your hands very quickly. So it is not a bad idea when you're working these light-colored woods to wash your hands frequently so as not to transfer dust and dirt from your workbench. A clean work surface also helps! When you sharpen your tool, wash your hands to remove the oil, because this would be a disaster on your wood.

Dirt is very difficult to remove from oak; you can scrape it out or you can try scrubbing it with water, mild detergent, and a brush, but you will always have

5-22. Deep undercutting is very effective.

some residual discoloration. You will also probably get discoloration from the water detergent or the soap that you use.

In terms of surface finish we have already said that the wood's being as hard as it is makes it difficult to achieve a very smooth surface. Oak responds quite well visually with residual chisel marks, so that it can have a nice hand-done "off the tool" look. If you use an abrasive paper you'll certainly get a very smooth surface, but the open, grainy nature of the wood makes the sanded surface look very much as though that is exactly what's been done to it. It looks artificial. So in a sense a chiseled surface with some residual facets on it is quite attractive to the eye and makes quite a pleasing surface finish to the carving. Here we have a case where the wood or the medium itself starts to dictate to us in fairly certain terms the kinds of finish that look best on it. The wood actually tells you what it wants you to do to it. You could seal the surface with a clear sealer, and then apply wax furniture polish.

chapter 6

THE ART OF REPEATING SOMEONE ELSE'S MISTAKES

Colonial Reproduction

The faithful reproduction is an art in itself! To do it one must avoid the temptation to make things "better." We are duplicating someone else's work, so we must pretend we are they and do it "their way." We need to develop an understanding of why things are the way they are in someone else's carving, how the person "got there," and why we are doing the reproduction in the first place.

The trouble with art is that everyone looking at it is an art critic. The trouble with artists is that they are the harshest critics of all! So, when a woodcarver with even just a little experience looks at someone else's carving, there is always something he or she would have done differently.

Now, there is nothing especially wrong with that, nothing wrong at all with a design improvement here or there, or an application of better technique, or just a change that personalizes the appearance of the work. Except in one of the following situations:

If you need to repair a carving, restore it, or replace it completely with one that looks the same, then you must develop the ability to reproduce the carving as it was, so that the "look" is the same as the original. If it is a repair, and your work doesn't "fit" with the original, your work will stand out and make the overall impact somewhat disappointing.

If it is a replacement of a whole item, you may "get away" with a different "look" provided the item isn't seen in close proximity to a similar one that was carved by the same person. The closer the carvings are physically to one another, the easier and more likely that automatic comparisons will be made. Two slightly different door panels side by side on the same door will be pretty obviously not the same. The same two door panels at either end of the room won't be nearly so obviously different, if ever at all.

If a reproduction of an original is the requirement, there is little point in arguing the merits or otherwise of the original artwork. If, in your opinion, something is glaringly wrong, then you must be glaringly wrong too. There is no room for your artistic pride, other than your pride in faithfully reproducing someone else's "mistakes"! The hardest thing of all, in fact, will be putting up with the criticism of others—"This should have been like that" or "That's not how you do it, you're supposed to do it like this." So you need to "stick to your guns," as the saying goes, and keep cool in heat of the critic's commentary.

How do we go about achieving someone else's art? We will take the example of a "folk"-style door panel from a kitchen cabinet that could be found anywhere in Europe or North America, or Australia. We will analyze it and see just what it is we have to do to make ours look the same. In doing so, we will also take a look at an execution that is an "improvement," and compare the two from an aesthetic point of view.

But before we do, here is an example of how a "homemade" restoration tricked local council building inspectors into thinking that a set of brand-new

6-1. Architectural carving must be in keeping with the overall feel of the building.

gable ends were the originals and therefore had "heritage protection." The before and after look at the completion of a new installation are shown in 6-1 and 6-2. Notice the difference color makes in shadow intensity.

In this example, the house was built in 1879 and is of Victorian Italianate style.

It is a simple cottage without the pretensions of grandiose architecture or wealth, built in the pioneering days of the suburb (in Sydney, Australia) where it stands today. Tools were very limited to the builders of this house, and materials and techniques used were equally basic. And therein lies the key to making new gable ends look as thought they were the originals of 120 years ago.

The trick is not to get too clever and sophisticated with design or workmanship. So, don't use electric sanders to get a perfect smoothness. Don't spend days doing the chisel work to such a degree of perfection that the boards should be French polished instead of painted! They must look hand-done, be a bit rough without being coarse and unpleasantly sloppy, and have a few chisel facets left to add to the "handmade character." The façade of this house isn't perfect—it is of rendered 10-in (255mm) handmade sand-stock brick walls. So it is important that the carving isn't perfect either. Imperfect in this case looks good.

6-2. The lighter color makes the shadows more visible.

Perfection would be quite out of place and look odd. Certainly it wouldn't look "original." When the house was re-roofed recently, the inspectors photographed the old gable ends before commencement of the restoration to ensure they were replaced when the new roof went on. The gable ends were "valuable heritage items." What the inspectors didn't know was that they were about 115 years younger than the heritage claimed them to be.

6-3. How many "faults" can you find with this carving?

Kitchen Door Panel

Let's turn now to the kitchen cabinet door panel—it might just have come from the house we've been talking about. The original is of oak, and our copies are of meranti, dressed to 6 in × ½ in × 15 in (150mm × 13mm × 380mm). Here are some of the things that are "wrong" with our model, shown in 6-3. See if you can find some more—and as you do it, and as you check out this list, try to get a feel for the "flavor" of the carving. A little later we will see what it looks like with most of these things "fixed":

✳ The scrolls in the left- and right-hand bottom corners are different sizes.
✳ The background is uneven and lumpy. It has been stamped to break up its rough appearance—a common practice for those in a hurry. Mind you, it is not a bad effect anyway!
✳ The leaf pattern on the right-hand side of an imaginary center line is not the same as the left—very little is symmetrical.
✳ The borders are not straight and square.
✳ The "V" grooves that perhaps should be matched pairs are of uneven lengths and go in different directions.
✳ You can see chisel (gouge) cuts in the pattern that appear as careless mistakes.

All in all, if you want to be critical, there is plenty to write about. However, our objective isn't to be critical, it is to work out how to best recreate the original artist's carving. We have done a six-point artistic examination, but this doesn't tell us anything much about how to copy what was done. So now let us reexamine the carving, from the point of view of the practical issues of reproduction:

✳ THE CARVER'S TOOLS WERE SHARP AND HE OR SHE USED A MALLET
We can deduce this because the carving was done in European oak, a relatively hard wood, and each of the vertical gouge cuts is very positive and clean. There is no evidence of multiple attempts to make a cut. To do this, a mallet is necessary in this wood, and the tools must be sharp, or there will be tearing and/or multiple attempts will be needed. You can tell if more than one attempt was made; if this were the case, there would likely be one or more ridges where the cutting end of the blade stopped after each mallet blow and the next cut started.

✳ THE ORIGINAL CARVING WAS MOST LIKELY DONE VERY MUCH WITH PRICE IN MIND, AS IT WAS CARVED QUICKLY AND WITH ONLY A FEW TOOLS
If you examine the curves in the carving, you will see that there are only two different ones. Make a template of one curve, and see where you can match it on the carving. You will only need two templates to cover the entire work. A V-tool was used for the "grooving"; a flatter tool was used for the background, which was also stamped with a background punch to disguise the "mess" of the uneven depth of the grounding. Four carving tools are all that were used, plus a mallet.

✳ THE CARVER ALSO PROBABLY DID IT FROM MEMORY
This is probable because of the asymmetry of the carving. It is likely that the pattern was not drawn on the wood before carving began, because many of the elements of the work are not the same on the left and right sides. If it were drawn on, the carver would have been automatically more careful to get things the

same. One of the key things about this kind of carving is its spontaneity—it just happens without a lot of prior planning. Sometimes this lack of planning and the speed with which the carving is done are to its detriment—it just becomes untidy, a bit like this example. There is a balance needed to maintain both the pleasing nature of spontaneity and the desire for quality.

So let us take a look at how we might go about reproducing some of these shapes. Consider 6-4. The carver chose a gouge that in his or her mind was the curve needed to create the scroll. A stop-cut was punched in with a mallet, making a vertical cut around the scroll. Presumably the same gouge was then used to put in the clearing cut at about 45 degrees to meet the stop-cut.

Unfortunately, the sweep of the gouge wasn't quite broad enough for the curved edge that goes up to the left end of the carving, so there is a "scallop" that breaks the continuity of the curve clearly visible opposite the scroll itself. A more perfect carving would have had this curve evened out to a continuous sweep. If you look across to the right of 6-4, you will see that same "scallop" to the left of the scroll. Unless you want these irregularities to be there, it is important to choose a different gouge, modify the curve to suit, or adjust the carving to remove them. If you decide to leave them in, it should be because they are part of the design (as they are in this reproduction). This interrupted curve is a definite and significant fault in the appearance of the work. In this case of reproduction, the discipline isn't to ensure they are removed, but indeed to leave them in! Clearly the sweep of the curve we have just been talking about was also too broad to fit within the border, so that at each end it became flattened.

Some other classics of uncontrolled tool work are highlighted in 6-5. We can clearly see the results of poorly controlled V-tool activity. The grooved arcs are very irregular sweeps.

6-4. For accurate reproduction do not remove the scallop on the sweep that moves upwards to the left from the scroll, no matter how ugly it may look.

6-5. Very irregular grooves might also be ugly, but they are a part of the original and must be reproduced. You could try using a blunt tool.

The close-up 6-6 shows many irregularities. Misplaced stop-cuts, and untidy edges and grooves, are quite visible. You will need to have a background punch to stamp the rough background.

To get your carving underway, the easiest thing to do is to place some tracing paper over the original panel, draw on the pattern, and then transfer it to the wood with carbon paper. The carving is fairly flat, so tracing is easy. Touch up any parts that need adjusting with freehand sketching. For a deeper relief where tracing is inappropriate, enlarge a photograph on a scanner/PC or photocopying system, and then transfer to the wood.

6-6. The stop-cut cutting into the pattern must be reproduced. The background stamp looks to be from a nine-pointed punch.

6-7. *Trace directly onto tracing paper and transfer with carbon paper. These instructions won't mean anything to anyone except the originator.*

6-8. *These panels were carved from the tracing done for 6-7. They would live very harmoniously with the original in 6-3.*

One carver's transfer from a tracing is shown in 6-7, together with some instructions to himself. These instructions would need to be made a lot clearer if they were for anyone else to follow. The finished work is shown in 6-8, where the carver actually did a double panel for a door. We see a well-balanced execution, complete with the odd chipping here and there on the edges. The V-tool work is certainly irregular, and the gouge cuts around the scrolls are not clean. The irregularity of the sweep we spoke about for creating the scallops is well executed, although generally the curves are too neat in this reproduction—they are all different shapes in the original. This carver thought about them, to his detriment, whereas the original carver didn't. Another key difference from the original is that the background is very flat. The original is very lumpy and disorganized—typical of the kind of background that was stamped to disguise the mess. Of course, what is missing is the aged look—some dark varnish would complete the picture.

In 6-9 we see a case of the carver going a bit too far on the untidy side. Now, to be fair, it is very difficult to find the balance and deliberately make mistakes when the very thing one tries to learn is to do the opposite. Deliberately muck it up? Very difficult! The main "problem" with this example is that the cuts are not clean—at least in the original the gouge incisions were mostly precise and well executed. The carving was done in a hurry, yes, but by a carver who certainly had the skills to make clean, precise cuts, even if they weren't all quite in the right place. It would not be unreasonable to decide that this carver had not yet developed the skills to make clean, positive cuts—particularly as the wood used for this carving is meranti, which is considerably easier to work than the

European oak of the original. The accidental chisel cut in the bottom right corner is a good example of how apparent inexperience can indeed add to the "flavor" of the moment, although it is not present on the original. It does, in its own way, "fit into" the reproduction concept.

While we are on the subject of wood, the degree of difficulty of reproducing a similar "look" in a wood different from the original is quite high. These examples illustrate the point quite clearly. Meranti is, in comparison to oak, quite soft and stringy. It can tear easily and can be woolly, whereas oak is generally the opposite.

Obviously, if the new carving is to be mounted as a replacement for the original, then the correct wood must be chosen. For this exercise we deliberately used what is in many ways a more difficult wood, to make the learning curve that much steeper.

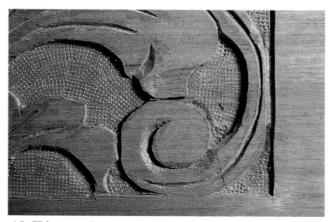

6-9. *This carver has gone too far on the messy side.*

6-10. The concave chamfers in the bottom right-hand quadrant are scalloped badly, whereas the original is done in a single cut.

6-11. Lines that are too clean, a background too well presented, make for something premeditated rather than spontaneous.

Another double panel is seen in 6-10, another creditable student effort, where we again see the results of the stringy and woolly nature of the meranti. There is also uncertainty evident in this carving that is not in the original. This expresses itself as a series of scallops made with the gouge along the clearing cuts in the bottom right-hand quadrant. You can see the scallop shadows, whereas a more experienced carver would have made a single cut along the curve. The background punch is also a little on the fine side.

We can see in 6-11 a spontaneity not present in 6-8, 6-9, or 6-10. To get this feel, you need a confident hand, tempered by speed—and by a lack of desire to do a great job! In other words you need to be able to do it, but not want to.

In 6-12 we have something approaching a real conflict of interest. The "line work" with the V-tool certainly has a flavor similar to the original, and the gouge cuts are certainly clean and well executed. The scrolls aren't the same size, and there are one or two gouge cuts that shouldn't be there. A pretty good effort? Yes, it certainly is, except there is one thing really wrong with it: It has the mechanical elements of the right flavor, but it is too good. It is too clean. Too premeditated. Not spontaneous poor quality. And that is the essence of this reproduction—to be able to carve spontaneous poor quality.

Compare 6-3 and 6-12 again. One of the real "give-aways" is the very well-organized background in 6-12. So flat, so neat, so well presented. Look again at the absolute disaster of the background of the original, which gives it all the character that it has. Horrible? Sure. But it looks so good, doesn't it?

By now all those seeking aesthetic beauty will be up in arms about how something so bad could be described as looking so good. That is the wonder of art, isn't it?

No matter what is expressed by whom, no matter whether it is considered good, bad, or indifferent by whom, just try to copy it and you will discover that someone else's art is their very own and defies casual reproduction.

6-12. A good example of reproduction, showing part of the background before stamping.

chapter 7

OVER AND OVER

Frames and Borders

Let's consider picture frames, box lids, and breadboards, even architraves and mantel pieces. The repetitive pattern is one of the oldest styles of carving, and one that has probably seen more applications than any other form. There are many "traditional" patterns like egg and dart, ribbon and leaf, bead or berry and sausage, floral motifs of all kinds, Celtic motifs, and even the candy twist—although this is probably more correctly continuous rather than repetitive. Whatever your definition, all these kinds of pattern have one thing in common: If you can do it once, you need to do it twice. And then over, and over, and over again!

And that is the key—your ability to successfully produce repetition. Boring? Maybe. Depends on your outlook. There is one amazing thing, though, about doing the same thing twice—and that is simply that you did it! Taking it further, if it looks great the first time and great the second and the third and every other time, then it means you have mastered skill and technique—and that means you are well on the way to doing some very clever things in your carving career. You will be able to do things without thinking about them. The things you do will become second nature to you, and from that moment on you will experience the explosion of a discovery curve that will surprise you, thrill you, and give you a whole new impetus. So much for being boring! Try it! Do the exact same thing successfully over and over. You'll see what we mean. Especially when you go to do something different. You will take it on with an entirely different outlook—you will want to do that twice too!

The Process

So, how do we do it? The first requirement is that you want to do it. Now, that may sound like a patronizing oversimplification, but in reality it is the truth. If you don't want to, then most likely you never will, or you will do it poorly. If you really want to, then the rest is not a great deal more than the application of some straightforward principles:

You must have accurate templates that will last the distance. Don't use cardboard that is too flimsy, as the edges will damage. Sheets of plastic for stenciling may be available to you, or you could cut your templates from acetate that might be used for map reading or navigation or be discarded from packaging of some kind. You could use a stencil-cutting knife, which has a fine, very small blade that rotates 360 degrees to make it easier to cut around corners.

Your wood must be correctly prepared—the molding must be accurately cut. This could be done with a router or hand molding planes.

Make sure you have the correct tools for the job. Often it is possible to compromise; however, with repetitive work it becomes too much of a trial to be continuously "making do," and your work will deteriorate as a result. For these carvings you will need a skew and a ¼-in (6mm) relatively flat gouge.

You must be in an environment and frame of mind that are conducive to accurate repetitive actions. It is too easy to have everything going along smoothly, and all of a sudden you miss a beat and you start to shape something differently or leave something out or get things in the wrong order. This is especially so in the marking-out phase. This happens if you are too tired, can't keep your mind on what you are doing, or are interrupted or distracted.

You must use templates or be skilled at freehand drawing.

Preparation of Stock Using Hand Molding Planes

Before any actual carving takes place, it is essential that the stock be carefully prepared. The cross section must be right-angular, the faces and edges perfectly flat. Test also for wind with winding sticks, particularly if the run is long. It is very difficult if not impossible to create a picture frame, for example, with twisted stock. You certainly won't want to do your carving and then discover that the surface isn't level. Jelutong is used in these examples. You could also use lime or basswood.

For the Berry and Sausage

The shape for the cross section is shown in 7-1. The wood is dressed to ⅝ in × ½ in (16mm × 13mm) and then rabbeted ⁵⁄₁₆ in (8mm) deep and ⅛ in (3mm) wide. It is important to consider the practicalities of making the stock before you embark on this sort of project. If you have milling equipment, then you may well have the cutters to make it mechanically. Otherwise, you will need at least a rabbet plane and prefer-

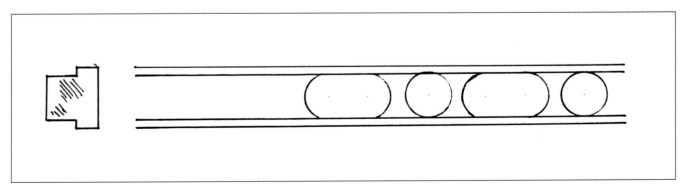

7-1. Choose a length of stock that is convenient to use for your berry and sausage. Under 20 in (500mm) is probably too awkward.

7-2. *Be certain your cutting blade and height-stop are set correctly. Hold the plane in a relaxed manner, vertically, and apply gentle pressure diagonally in towards the middle of the strip as you push the plane forward.*

ably also a plow plane. The easiest way to make the stock for the berry and sausage is to start with a wide board dressed to ⅝ in (16mm). Hold it between bench dogs or mount it on a wide board with a cleat along the edge and a stop at the end, like a long, narrow bench hook. Rabbet one edge, and then with the plow plane cut a groove with the shoulder at ⅝ in (16mm), which is the required width of stock for the berry/sausage. Make the groove with the plow plane twice the width of the rabbet plus the kerf of the saw you will use to rip it. If you cut it carefully down the center of the groove, you will have the rabbet for an additional length already made.

If you prepare the stock to the required thickness and width before you rabbet the edges, it will be too narrow and flexible to put between bench dogs—the wood strip will spring and be impossible to work.

How to hold a rabbet plane is shown in 7-2. Note that, just as with your carving tools, it is important to have a comfortable and relaxed posture for your hands. You will also see that the middle, ring, and little fingers of the right hand are gently helping to hold the plane in against the strip.

For the Ribbon and Leaf

The cross section for the ribbon and leaf is shown in 7-3. The wood is dressed to 2 in × ¾ in (50mm × 20mm), then rabbeted ⅝ in (16mm) deep and 5⁄16 in (8mm) wide before the top is molded into the curve with the molding plane. The stock for this is stable enough to hold between bench dogs without springing. If you don't have that facility, once again hold it on a wider baseboard with a cleat tacked to it along its length, add an end stop to prevent the strip from sliding, and clamp the base board to your bench. First rabbet each side of the strip, and then use your hollow plane to create the curved top.

How to hold the molding plane is shown in 7-4. Once again you should notice the relaxed posture of the hands. The curved shape of the top is shown in 7-5. The end stop is not shown, so that you can get a clear view.

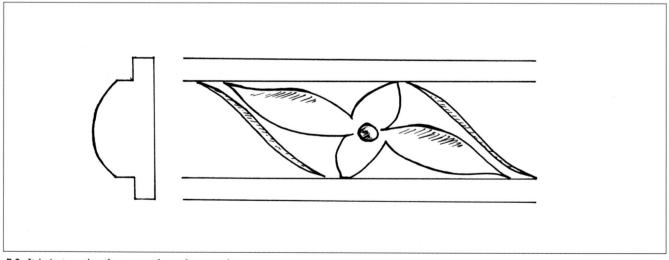

7-3. *It is imperative that your planes be very sharp.*
Test them on scrap before you start, to make sure there is no surface tearing.

7-4. The curved "hollow" in the end of the blade must exactly match the hollow in the wooden sole of the plane. If they do not match, you must regrind the blade to the correct shape, otherwise the cutting blade cannot work.

7-5. Careless marking out can be a source of great frustration.

7-6. Compass points could cause permanent damage to the wood. A template is the only safe marking method. The stop-cuts have been done with a skew—but a curved gouge is better (see 7-8).

7-7. A gouge upside down only works if you have the right shape for the work.

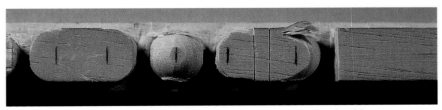

7-8. Make a curved stop-cut at the ends of the sausages and the beads with an appropriately curved gouge.

Carving Beads and Sausages

A typical mistake when marking out is shown in 7-6; it could ruin your stock. Concentration lapsed, and all of a sudden there were two beads being set up in a row. Not only that, they would not even be the same size—not that that would have mattered much!

In 7-7 you can also see the trouble you could get into if you do not use a template. In this case, the carver used a compass to mark out the circles, and in doing so put a pinhole at every center. This now needs to be carved off—and that will unfortunately lower the height of each bead.

If you consider making the berry-and-sausage pattern by using a gouge upside down, then make very sure that you choose a tool that really is the correct shape. For example, you can see in 7-8 what can happen if the curve of the tool is slightly too tight for the curve of the berry. The shoulders have dug into the "circle" and the net effect will be a significant reduction in the size of the finished berry.

7-9. Your skew can be used as a scraper, and you could lightly undercut for effect. A fine abrasive paper creates a nice finish.

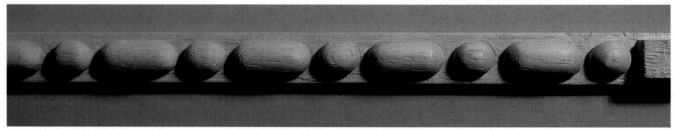

7-10. Be sure you have thought through your layout. If you are doing a frame, draft a life-size mock-up on paper to be sure the pattern length and miter joints are properly accommodated.

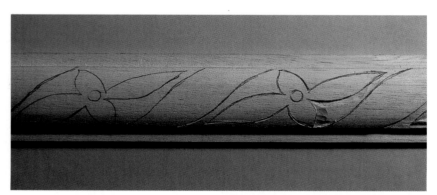

7-11. You may get a more uniform result if you carve common parts of each repeat of the pattern at the same time, rather than each leaf separately.

7-12. If your border is to be painted or gilded, you may need to carve it differently to allow for thick coatings.

The examples in 7-9 and 7-10 were done with a skew. First, cut between each berry and sausage with a tenon saw, remove the waste between each with the skew, and then continue to shape them with the same tool. The cuts between the bead and sausage in 7-7 were made with a coping saw, which is a more cumbersome activity.

Carving the Ribbon and Leaf

For the ribbon and leaf, first create the leaves and expose the ribbon by removing the waste between them; then shape the insides of the leaves, exposing the bead in the center, and then make this round with the skew. 7-11 and 7-12 show this progressively.

Your skew and a relatively flat ¼-in (6mm) gouge are all you should need. Unless you are very skilled at repetitive freehand drawing, a template is essential. If you have done the exercises in Chapter 5, this carving is very straight-forward. Accurate marking out is about the most difficult part.

Borders for frames are often painted or gilded with metal leaf. It is important that you consider the proposed surface finish before you get too advanced with your carving, as it may be that the finish will have an impact on your style of carving.

For example, if you are going to paint the work, and depending on the kind of paint finish you want, you will need to imagine that there are a sealer, undercoat, and maybe two top coats over the carving. These coatings will add a thickness over the surface that will inevitably affect the amount of shadow your carving creates. Nice, fine shadows around an edge may well be filled in with paint, and not be there at all at the end. Undercutting might be a waste of time, or alternatively it might need to be deeper in order to accommodate the paint and still create a shadow. The best thing to do is to experiment with the carving and the finish. Do a leaf or two and cover them with your proposed finish, and assess whether it is really what you want before you launch into spending hours that might not give you a satisfying look.

Similarly, if you are to gild the frame, be very careful about the thickness of the surface coating. Gilding can easily add a millimeter of thickness and alter the look considerably. If you are going to have a gilder do the work for you, do your carving only after you have discussed it with the craftsman. Aspects such as undercutting in various circumstances are quite inappropriate for gilding purposes, and you will probably find the gilder will fill them with gesso, a surface coating made from chalk whiting and animal glue.

A completed leaf is shown in 7-13. A gilder would seal the surface of the porous jelutong and apply several coats of gesso, creating a very smooth base for gold leaf. The chips would disappear, as would the internal checking you can see at the top of the running along the rim. What would also disappear is the nice strong shadow on the edge of the ribbon to the left of the leaf. It would be very dull—if it didn't get filled in altogether with gesso! Gold leaf doesn't go over corners very well, so the gilder is looking to create smooth surfaces with no angular parts that might make the process impossible.

7-13. A gilder would seal the surface of the porous jelutong of the completed leaf and apply several coats of gesso, creating a very smooth base for gold leaf. The chips would disappear, as would the internal checking you can see at the top, running along the rim.

chapter 8

A RENAISSANCE FOR YOUR SKILLS

*Renaissance-
Style
Pediment*

In this chapter we will start to look at design and the development of it from basic line drawings. Each of the examples is taken from work completed by students in their first extensive exercise of line-drawing interpretation and development. While the carving itself is not especially difficult for an experienced carver, what we have chosen is reasonably complex from the development point of view, and the decisions that need to be made are many and varied. Part of the study in this carving is also to get the right-hand side of the carving to look as close as possible to the left-hand side.

Honduras mahogany is prepared to 10 in × 1⅛ in × 23½ in (250mm × 30mm × 600mm). You could also use walnut, maple, or rosewood. The line drawing for the pediment is shown in 8-1, together with some instructions a carver has written. In this example of the preparation of instructions there are some very typical errors that are a common trap for the inexperienced. It is very important when you are in your planning phase, and writing instructions for yourself, to be sure you think ahead in terms of being able to actually create what your instructions say. Now, this might seem a bit obvious, but be assured what we are about to point out is very often the kind of thing that is written down.

1 The instructions indicate that the foliage at the top of the head is to be convex in form. If the foliage itself is to be convex, how is the inside of it convex as well? This is achievable only with great difficulty with the foliage behind the knob at the left of the head. The areas are so small that it would be basically impossible to do, unless the inside of the foliage is raised above the perimeter—which is not likely to be the intention of the drawer. Certainly the instructions don't say that. Would it not be better for this background to be flat?

2 Similarly, are we are to carve two concave forms on either side of the curved line (which would become a ridge) on the forehead, or is the whole of that area concave with the line an incised marking? It would be reasonable to assume the line represents an incised marking, but it is unclear.

3 Diagonally left of the eye, we see there are two different forms meeting one another. There is the concave shape to the left and the convex to the right. How does this work? What happens where the two shapes meet? It is not impossible to do, but there may well be some aesthetic issues to be considered. It might look fairly odd.

4 In the center of the nose, we have a notation that there is to be a visible ridgeline. But is this to be all the way from the bottom to the top of the carving? All the way through the mouth, the forehead, and the foliage on top of the head? This would be a fairly unlikely outcome, although that is what this vertical line indicates. What is most likely to be the case is that the line going through the middle of the drawing represents exactly that—the middle of the proposed carving. In which case the person writing the instructions simply adopted it as the "ridgeline" and wrote the instruction accordingly, creating what is a fundamental error inasmuch as it cannot be carved.

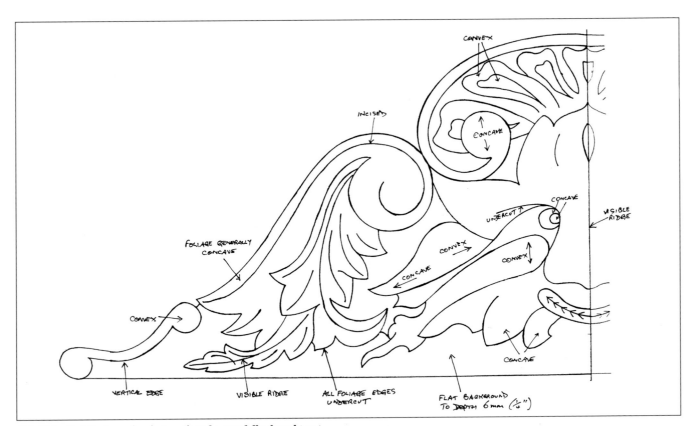

8-1. It is vital that carving instructions be carefully thought out. Poor prior planning can end in errors that are impossible to fix.

8-2. Variation in the depth of the carving is an important part of the development of flow movement and shadow.

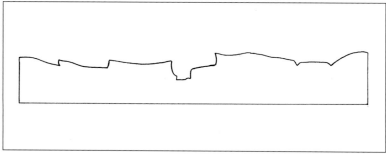

8-3. This is the profile horizontally from the eye.

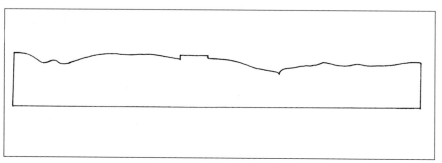

8-4. This is the profile horizontally from the nostril.

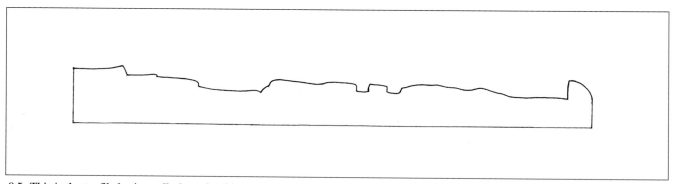

8-5. This is the profile horizontally from the chin.

It is very important to think somewhat more carefully about the proposed carving. It is not good enough to do sloppy planning, because once the carving is underway it is often impossible to correct such fundamentally wrong design features. A bad mistake very early in the work can ruin the chances of a good or even reasonable result in the end. Thorough prior planning is just as important as the work itself.

Another aspect of this carving is that we need to make both sides of the work resemble one another as closely as possible. This in itself is not necessarily an easy task, and requires some careful planning to execute. This makes it all the more important to have a good, clear set of instructions—or forward plan—for yourself right from the outset. If you start one side and it doesn't work out too well, and you correct it on the other side, you can well imagine the potential mess you could get into.

In order to get the feeling of flow and movement in the work, it is important to make sure there is sufficient variation in the depth of the carving across its main features. Consider 8-2. We see a puffy bulk around the cheek area, with the foliage falling away to the left so that the depth from the top of the carving to the background is 15mm at the cheek and 6mm at the end of the left-hand leaf.

Decorative Woodcarving

To make this easier to understand, it is worth taking some time to study and understand the profile drawings shown in 8-3, 8-4, and 8-5. Each of these sketches represents the profile, first horizontal through from the eye, then from the nostril, and third from the chin. It is important to study these as they give you a clear idea of the changes in the depth of the carving. It is these changes that help give the carving the flow and movement mentioned earlier. Try to follow these profiles and compare them to the photograph of the carving. In a few minutes you will see how they work—at the right-hand end of each sketch the carving is 1⅛ in (30mm) thick, and at the left-hand end it is 1 in (25mm) thick. Therefore the border or perimeter of the carving is lower than the center. If you do not quite see in your mind's eye how you want to do a carving, then you will find that this technique will assist you greatly in organizing your thinking.

You don't need to do profiles for the whole of the carving, but for those areas that you find hard to follow. It is the extension of the technique discussed in Chapter 4, "Of Course You Can Draw." You may also find profile drawings useful if you wish to explain to a client what a shape will look like.

Note on the line drawing in 8-1 that there is no rendition of the foliage below the chin—it is missing. The design would look rather odd without it, so it is necessary to put it in. These are typical of the sorts of error that are found when you start to study drawings—never assume it is all there and in fact always assume it is not, and you will deliberately go looking for errors, and undoubtedly find something you are not altogether happy with.

Starting with 8-2, we will first look at style. This unfinished example is set up to demonstrate the crispness and clarity that can be achieved in Honduras mahogany, and how the original drawing can be modified to give more life to the foliage than the version the drawing would have produced. All of this is a matter of opinion and imagination; however, as a general rule the amount of life and vitality of a carving with foliage is a function of clarity and sharpness rather than roundness,` which tends to produce a softer vision. 8-6 is an example of this. We discuss this again towards the end of the chapter.

When you start to do the carving, it is one of the objectives to get both halves looking the same as one another, so you need to develop a "system" and use it in a disciplined and systematic fashion. You will probably find that, if you work a few minutes on one half and then move to the corresponding area of the other half and work it to the same stage, this will be easiest. Don't make the work periods too short—you are the best judge of what is long or short, but maybe 15 minutes a side is good enough to start. If you make the work periods too long, you will advance the carving too much to make it an easy copy for the other side.

The other skill you will start to find particularly useful is an ability to be ambidextrous. It has not been especially important up until now; however, you will find it very useful for this duplicating process. Do a small amount of carving on one side, swap hands, and complete the mirror image on the other. This is a very convenient and time-saving skill to develop. Either that or you will need to continuously turn your carving around or walk around it, so the sooner ambidexterity is practiced and developed the better. This is for two reasons; the sooner your carving becomes easier to do there will be much greater work satisfaction, and probably more important, the best time to train your brain for this until-now-unnatural activity is when your brain is scrambling to understand and do the new things you keep placing before it. Get in early with what might seem the most non-learnable skill, and you might just be surprised at what becomes reality. It is also not uncommon for people who are right-handed to suddenly find they are able to do a new skill better left-handed, and vice versa. Most people should find it very easy to be ambidextrous without a mallet, whereas to effectively use a mallet right- or left-handed might take a little longer.

8-6. This example lacks crispness, makes detail soft and vague.

8-7. Disorganized ribs or veins and indecisive shapes create an untidy appearance.

8-8. This is the bottom left-hand section of 8-1, interpreted differently in every example shown.

8-9. Not exactly how the drawing said it should be; however, clarity and positive direction are certainly present.

In the process of the determination of the "best" shapes for components such as the foliage, it is important to consider the overall look that you wish to achieve. If you are unsure what this actually is—and this is most likely the case if you are not experienced at this sort of thing—then don't worry about it, simply experiment. Take an off-cut of the wood you are working in, and draw the foliage two or three different ways to see which one you like the best. In the following examples, we will see some different executions of the same drawings, and you will see what we mean. First, let's look at a section of some foliage from the drawing, and two examples that have been carved:

The drawing calls for acutely serrated leaves with ribs that divide them into segments. Each of the two carvings has been done quite differently, with quite different results, primarily manifesting itself in a significantly different degree of clarity. In 8-7, there is a definite indecision as to where the serrations of the leaves should point. In the bottom left-hand corner they are all in different directions, compared to the corresponding part of either the drawing in 8-8 or the carving in 8-9. This has quite an impact on the appearance of the work.

Moving to the center of 8-8, we see that the carver has tried unsuccessfully to copy the drawing as far as the acute nature of the apex of the foliage is concerned. This is the point in the middle where the strands of foliage meet. The rib in the center drifts away to the right in an awkward manner. The carver in 8-9, on the other hand, hasn't followed the drawing closely at all, although the ridges for the ribs are clean, well placed, and create a strong shadow up through the center of the leaf. The choice of concave shapes at either side of the mid-vein also creates a combination of shadows that is more effective than those in 8-8.

Clearly, then, the choices open to the carver are many and varied, and the subsequent decisions made will have a major effect on the outcome. A simple drawing can lead to a long list of alternatives, each offering a different potential result. And, as we said a little earlier, if you are in doubt as to what to do, then experiment!

Let's look at another set of variations that make for substantially different results. The scroll that is to be done on either end of the pediment is shown in the drawing as a plain and essentially nondescript decoration. Here is what four different people did with it:

The carving seen in 8-10 is the one obviously closest to the original drawing. Nicely smooth all over, it has one major drawback—and that is the clarity or sharpness of the image of the actual scroll. Compare the "knobby" part in 8-10 to that in 8-12. While 8-12 is a different style of execution altogether, you can see the clarity of the perimeter, which is of the same dimension as that in 8-10. The corner of the scroll needs to be tucked in as though it were actually going around in a scrolling motion—not rounded off and softened as though it were intended to be a blurry blob.

This issue of clarity is of exceptional importance—it is of the same importance as the making of a straight line that isn't crooked or a beautiful sweeping curve that hasn't a kink in it. The errors are very obvious and very irritating. One might even say disturbing, certainly to the "expert" eye. Poor clarity is born of a number of issues:

1 You must realize that clarity is there in the first place. Like all things, unless you are aware of it, you don't see it. Being aware is mostly a function of its being pointed out to you at the start—which is the easiest way to learn. If you don't know it could look better, it's natural to leave things how they are. To understand why poor clarity happens is equally important. 8-11 is an unsuccessful attempt to decorate the blob. The intent was there, but the clarity isn't.

2 The second most important reason is a lack of manual skill. Now, skill can only be developed, so it is again natural that in your early stages of carving you may lack the required practice and experimentation that will allow you to create a better kind of form. Often we find that the greatest impairment to skill development in carving is a kit of poorly sharpened tools—they will hold you back to such an extent as to make it almost improbable that you ever move very far forward.

3 Do make sure that your tools are very finely polished. A sharp tool will let you do things that you otherwise would not be able to do. If you can't achieve a crisp undercut with a blunt tool, and that is all you have, then no amount of practice will do you any good at all. 8-12 and 8-13 have been done with sharp tools, and are two quite different but nonetheless effective executions.

8-10. Without the scroll end's being "tucked in," the result is a bit like a blob.

8-11. Poor definition spoiled these scroll ends.

8-12. Sharp tools and a purposefulness give a much more pleasing result.

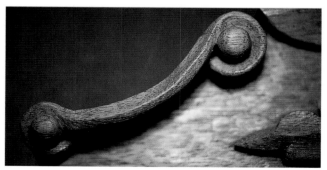

8-13. These scrolls have a hand-done feeling, giving a warm touch.

8-14. Too much shine, too many flat surfaces, and those eyes?

8-15. Be very careful of those dirty hands—wood loves dirt!

4 Correct and effective lighting for the creation of shadows will let you see what you are doing. Good cross lighting will let you see shapes clearly, and if you have any doubts about your eyes, then have them tested by a qualified practitioner. This is not a bad thing to do in any case when starting a new visual activity. Not knowing our sight isn't perfect can create an environment where nothing will ever be right.

Let's turn now to four different executions of the remainder:

The first piece in 8-14 has a very shiny finish. It is a clear sealer and canauba wax, which gives a high sheen unsuitable to woodcarvings like this one. This unsuitability is due to the nature of shiny surfaces. They are designed to reflect light like a mirror, and if there is a large amount of curved surface, then there is a wide variety of reflected light in all directions, so that there tends to be an interruption to the visibility of the finished article. What you see is what you get: shine.

Apart from the shine on the surface of 8-14, a major criticism of it is that it's generally overall too flat. Note the nose, and the beads on all the scrolls. They are completely flat, whereas a rounded effect would be

visually much more appealing. The foliage is not as crisp as it could be, and there is little or no undercutting on the main surface areas to create the shadows we expect from well-defined relief carving.

You will also see that the light is picking up surfaces that are uneven. They have been cut with tools that are not sharp enough and the surfaces were sanded, then waxed. Sandpaper is not a substitute for poor gouge work. Sanding does not flatten small surface areas like the ones on this carving, it rounds them off. Sanding won't, unless you do a lot of it, remove the rough chisel work completely. There are a lot of residual rounded-off rough surfaces on this work, which you can compare to the crispness of a well-chiseled surface in 8-2.

In 8-15, we see fewer flat surfaces—compare noses for instance. The eyes are not quite so stark; and notice the difference when foliage is added below the chin. It was not in the original drawing and was left out in the carving of 8-14.

The other point worth noting is that in 8-15 we see the results of blunt chisels without the rough surfaces sanded off. You can see the furry edges on the foliage and the furry background behind the foliage above the head. The surface is also dirty, noticeable as a dull,

8-16. A different crown of foliage, and a different look altogether.

8-17. Sharp tools, positive cuts, and a pleasing result all round.

dark grayness. You can see it on the small scroll at the far right-hand end and on the perimeter above it. Dirty hands are a definite "NO" for woodcarving, dirt being very difficult to get out of the wood. Sometimes the tools being used will put a gray-black film on your hands, depending on the composition of the metal in the blade and your skin chemistry. Sweaty hands may cause this gray deposit to be transferred from the blade to you and then to the surface of the work. A dirty workbench will not help either.

We will look now at two further examples, which have quite different characteristics from the last two.

Notice the different approach to the foliage above the head on the carving in 8-16, and compare the eyes and the scrollwork to those in 8-14 and 8-15. The roundness of the surfaces and the crispness of the tool finish in both 8-16 and 8-17 indicate sharp tools well controlled, and patience to achieve a pleasing result.

If your tools are really sharp, you will notice that one immediate benefit is the pleasure you get from cutting the wood. And it is this pleasure that results in your having a greater desire to put in extra time to create your piece. If what you are doing looks good, you will want to spend time making it look even better. There is nothing worse than blunt tools for creating disenchantment.

Interestingly, in both 8-16 and 8-17 there is a fault in the sweep of the curve on the right cheek, just near the nose. The curve isn't clean in either case—there is a "kink" in it. With the lighting creating the shadows, it is very noticeable.

Areas on faces—such as eyes—are very significant focal points. You must take care to make sure that the surroundings are correct. Anywhere in the vicinity of a focal point, inadequate attention to detail will certainly be seen immediately.

chapter 9

SIGNPOST YOUR SUCCESS

Introduction to Lettering

With the exception of the "bead and sausage," the carving exercises so far described are for the most part arbitrarily compound curved surfaces that, provided they are formed within a framework of clarity and of acceptable design, will "look good." We have seen that no two people will necessarily carve exactly the same shape, but that the carvings can nevertheless look as good as one another, while originating from the same drawing.

In this chapter we will take a look at a very different proposition—that of the necessity for practiced precision. We have said before there is nothing worse than a crooked straight line or a circle that isn't. Added to this, you will have also found by now that there is nothing more frustrating than not being able to find the right tool for the job. In the examination of the requirements for both, we will look at some simple lettering, discuss some of the required techniques and tools, and make a specialist tool called a serif spade. A piece of scented rosewood dressed to 3½ in × 1 in × 23½ in (90mm × 25mm × 600mm) will comfortably accommodate the word "woodcarver" (see 9-1). You could also use mahogany or jelutong.

First, though, a refresher comment on lighting: If your workshop artificial light, or for that matter your natural light (if that is what you use), is not satisfactory, you will never achieve a high standard in this kind of carving. By "this kind" is meant those styles of carving that require crisp shadows to define uniformity of line and curve—chip carving would be a good generic-style type. It will be essential that you have clear, strong cross light in all directions (not all at once, but light you can move around or turn on and off). Remember that fluorescent lights are the worst because they don't cast a shadow of any consequence. You will need to be able to very clearly see the edges or shoulders of the letters in order to make sure they are not chipped or irregular, and the bottoms of the incising to make sure it is even in line or curve and cleanly cut, creating single, not multiple shadows.

9-1. In these two examples, both in Honduras mahogany, the shadow strength varies considerably, although in the bottom example the shadow is more uniform than in the top.

In Chapter 7, "Over and Over" we looked at setting out. With regard to lettering, setting out is equally important. In fact, if you wish to recreate a specific recognized font, then it will be necessary to observe the layout of the lettering for the typeface and match it correctly. It is not simply a matter of putting one letter next to another—the designer of the font will have deliberately chosen a format of relativity between each letter as an integral part of the design. In the example we will consider, the font is not a specific design.

As with the other carvings, the layout of the lettering may be traced or hand drawn, or a paper layout may be glued down onto the wood. The latter is not recommended, as the "template" will, at the edges of the letters, tend to rise off the wood or become frayed, making it difficult to carve correctly. Hand drawing the lettering directly onto the wood is the best method for accuracy. Be sure the wood is well prepared with a flat, unblemished surface. Do not sand it flat before you start to carve, otherwise you may incur tool damage from any residual abrasive grit. Sanding also changes the texture of the surface, tending to dull it. A sharp hand plane or a scraper is best.

You will need to decide the most appropriate depth to cut the letters, and this is best done with experimentation as well. Do a couple of different depths to assess the best result. Be careful not to make them too shallow, as you will not achieve a good shadow effect in that case. That is, unless you want them to look that way.

When choosing the wood for your sign, it is important that you select a wood that will give a crisp, clean finish and not be crumbly or furry at the edges. The best thing to do is to experiment with samples—do a part of a letter, or at least a straight section and a curved section, to test the ability of the wood to support the activity. Very open-grained woods are probably not a proposition, nor would be a stringy kind. If you want a sharp edge on the letters, then a wood prone to chipping may not be a proposition either. The only way to be really sure is to test a sample.

The majority of letters you will tackle will most likely be done with very few tools. You will certainly need a skew, a flat carpenter's chisel or carver's firmer chisel, and one or two gouges, and if your design has serifs as this one does, you will need to be able to cut them in with the appropriate tool. Whatever the case, unless your tools are very, very sharp, don't attempt lettering. The principles to follow are quite simple:

✳ cut cleanly,

✳ cut crisply, and

✳ cut the right shape in the right place.

Key Issues

We are not going to look at design in this chapter, nor are we to examine setting out. We will, however, focus on the issues that affect precision of cutting.

Tool Sharpness

Make no mistake—if the tool you are using is not capable of precise incision in the wood you wish to work, then you will be incapable of producing the sharpness of image that is so pleasing with well-cut lettering. What we mean in effect by "sharpness of image" is "sharpness of shadow." If you end up with a blurred or inaccurate shadow, then you lose the impact you might have gained from the simplicity of precision. If you have any doubts at all, never hesitate for a second to work on your shortcomings. Never be too proud to ask someone else what he or she thinks of your experiments either—you'll be amazed at the kinds of thing you will learn. Many a time the other person's perception will be quite different from yours.

If you are creating incised lettering, it is important that the bottoms of the letters—the bottom of the "V" if that is the shape—be clean and neat. Otherwise you will ensure a blurry, untidy look that is not at all a very pleasing sight.

Tool Control

Second, there is the matter of tool control. We have said that before too. Now, as we have said, we are looking for precision with letter cutting. Control, therefore, is paramount. Each cut must be to the correct depth, the direction of each cut must be where it needs to be, and if two cuts need to meet in the middle, then that is what they should do, first go.

Control, as we have seen and by now experienced, comes from the equilibrium among ourselves, a sharp tool, our mallet if we are using one, and the wood we are carving. And this equilibrium can only come about through familiarity, and that occurs by practice. So here is a case where practice does make perfect. To make sure you are in control, before you start your lettering set up a practice board, and repeat, repeat, repeat.

You will need a mallet that is of the right density to help drive the tool cleanly to the correct depth in one

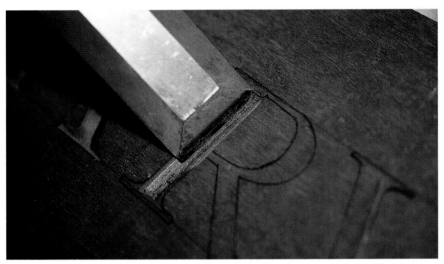

9-2. A carpenter's tool is handy for straight sections. Practice your cuts to minimize the number of strikes so the result is clean and not chewed up.

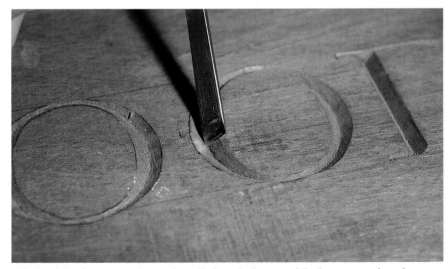

9-3. Don't let the corner of your skew dig into the bottom of the letter or cut into the opposite side.

go. The last thing you want is the little ridges that sometimes form along the side of the letter each time you strike the chisel. You won't want a mallet that is too heavy, nor one that is too light. Unfortunately there are no rules, and each of us is different, so you will have to experiment to find the correct weight for you. You must be comfortable in your posture and relaxed in your composure. Tension is the worst influence when you are trying to achieve tool control and precision.

Given this is the case, it is important to ensure you are very comfortable with the cutting activity you need to do, that you are well versed in it, and that it is definitely a part of your "repertoire."

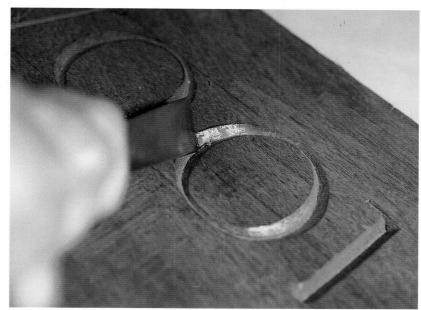

9-4. A very sharp gouge will help to ensure there is no chipping on the shoulders.

Things That May Happen

We will assume now that you have prepared your wood surface well, that your tools are sharp, and that the marking out is neat and tidy. In this example for the word "woodcarver," we are to cut in the letters in an incised "V" shape.

Taking a simple straight section of a letter, here are some of the options open to you for cutting it in, and some of the things that may happen to you:

❈ You may be tempted to use a V-tool to cut in the letter. This will be satisfactory up to a point, except when you get to the top or bottom of a part of the letter and there is a serif (the small flag-like tag)— or when you arrive at the junction of two parts such as the apexes in the letter "W," or when you find that the shoulders of the V-tool dig into one of the sides at the junction and damage it. Grinding the tool with raked-back shoulders so that the nose of the tool is sticking forward like the prow on a boat will help this, but it still leaves the actual corners unattended. If the apex of your V-tool is not a true "V" you may also have to recut the bottoms of the incisions.

If you do have the nose cut like a prow, this will allow your tool access to the corner, but will not solve the problem of how to cut the edges.

Using a parting tool will also dictate that both sides of the member are flat; and if you want one side flat and the other curved, it is of course impossible.

❈ You may decide to use a firmer chisel to cut in the edges. This will be fine for the majority of the letter's length, but once again it is inappropriate for the corners and serifs.

❈ You may use a skew to help cut in the corners and the serifs. This will do a reasonably good job, but you may find that the angle of the face of the skew makes it either awkward or simply too difficult to do.

❈ You will need to decide if the sides of the letters are to be flat, concave, or convex (this last would be quite difficult to do).

❈ You will need to establish, by experimentation, the best combination of gouge, skew, and firmer chisel work that suits the look you want (see 9-2, 9-3, and 9-4).

When it comes to the corners and junctions, one of the great disadvantages of the tools you will have in your kit is that they do most of the job, but do not allow you complete access to fulfill the cutting requirements.

One of the reasons for this is that the V-tool is very shape-specific, as are your gouges; and the skew, while being particularly versatile, is sometimes skewed too much for the activity at hand. Another reason why it is not completely satisfactory is the visibility it allows to the wood you are cutting. To see exactly and easily where you are going in relation to where you have come from is not always easy. It may be time, then, to modify an old tool and experiment a bit with a "new" design:

The shape we will make is known as a serif spade. It is specifically designed for cutting serifs; however, it is also very useful for other activities, as you will discover if you make one. What you need is a flat-faced firmer, say, about ⁵⁄₁₆ in (8mm) across for the letters in the example, which are 2 in (50mm) high. Grind the steel away from behind the corners, so that you expose them like tips, as in 9-5. It will be necessary to grind away the shaft as well, so that there is minimal steel to "get in the road."

If you have not done this sort of grinding before, there are some things you will need to watch:

✳ You must not let the steel get too hot, otherwise it will burn and become very fragile. Always have a tin of water next to your grinding wheel, and dip the tool in it frequently.

✳ You will see from 9-5 that this particular grinding has left a number of facets on the steel. It is a bit "all over the place." Now, this in itself is nothing other than an aesthetic objection, except of course if the facets are on the cutting edge. Provided the cutting edge is able to do its job, the rest doesn't really matter. Pretty tools don't guarantee pretty work. It is better, if time is limited, to spend it getting the edge right and the tool skills to a high standard.

9-5. Grinding slightly different shapes on each tip increases flexibility.

Note from 9-5 that the tips of the spade are not of the same shape—one is a little more elongated than the other. The reason for this is simply to increase the versatility of the tool with a longer tip that can get into different parts of the letter more easily than a thicker one. And, conversely, a thicker blade might sometimes be more useful than a thinner one.

Now, once you have made this "new" tool, you may well ask, Why this shape?

The only real way to find out is to use it. However, 9-6 and 9-7 give you an idea of its versatility. It really is pretty nifty! You will discover that you can see where you are going and where you have come from, that you can get into tight corners that you can't access with your skew, and that you can see what you are doing. The flat face is a distinct advantage over your skew for cleaning up the bottoms of the letters and rounding off the convex corners of the serifs.

9-6. Your serif spade will be handy for getting into all sorts of corner.

9-7. The great advantage of a tool this shape is you can see where you have been as well as where you are going.

9-8. *Just about everything that could go wrong has in this example. Precision can only be achieved by practice with the right tools that are very sharp.*

9-9. *What a difference the right combination makes. Even so, the serif at the top left of the "W" is crooked; and do you notice the jagged shadow at the apex of the same letter?*

You will find that if you grind the spade with a reasonably long flat bevel, with little or no convexity, it will be extremely useful for taking fine shavings and creating accurate and pleasing shapes. Do experiment with your tools to ensure you get the best results. What can happen when you don't is seen in 9-8, and 9-9 is when you do.

Use either your spade or skew or both to place a fine "push cut" in the bottom of the letters where the two sides meet, and this will give a neat trim that also places a shadow line at the base of the incision, ensuring a clean, crisp vision. You can see these shadows in 9-10.

Designing your own fonts can be fun, and it certainly helps you to understand how letters are constructed. Your personal computer has many different fonts you could experiment with for carving. 9-11 shows a pleasing personal touch.

The depth of the letters makes the shadow stronger as we can see in 9-12. In the top jelutong example, the shallow letters create a weaker vision than the mahogany. Depending on the color of the wood, the depth of the letters should be shallower or deeper, as indicated.

9-10. *The shadows are visible from the push cuts in the bottoms of the letters. The left-hand side of the letter "O" isn't quite right, and this creditable first effort was spoiled by not setting out the letters correctly. The carving nearly went off the end!*

9-11. *You can experiment also with your own designs, as did this carver. Notice the variation in shadow intensity, making things look uneven.*

9-12. *The depth of the letters makes the shadow stronger. In the top jelutong example, the shallow letters create a weaker vision than the mahogany.*

KEEP WITHYNNE COMPASSE, SO SHALL YE BE SURE

Gothic Tracery

So wrote Sir Robert William Billings in 1851 in *The Power of Form Applied to Geometric Tracery* (William Blackman and Sons, Edinburgh and London), referring, of course, to the basis for the form of tracery—the circle.

Pierced panels from history, with cusps, coves, foils, flutes, and sunken pockets, are the elements of gothic tracery. It is one of the most distinctive classic designs of all time. Gothic architecture is a style developed in northern France that spread through western Europe from the middle of the 12th century to the early 16th century. Ribbed vaulting, steep roofing, pointed arches, and tracery characterize it. Tracery is a geometric term and refers to the intersection of planes; in architecture it is the ornamental openwork at the head of a gothic window.

In artistic history, tracery of the Gothic architecture style probably had its origins in leaf foliage; indeed it consists mostly of three, four, or five foils, or leaves. If there is argument as to the correctness of this origin, so be it. So convinced was Sir Robert Billings that he wrote, "Let the skeptic examine the simple daisy, and if he be not convinced, then let him turn to the perfect geometric radiation of the cells of the sunflower. They are only equaled in geometric perfection by the hexagonal cell of that most industrious insect architect, the bee."

Whatever their correctness of history, we can be assured the various parts of the tracery have a name. If you refer to 10-1, the foil or leaf is the open black circular area between the two pairs of cusps that are the four pointed parts. The edges of the foils are chamfered with a concave curve, and the eyes (or sunken pockets) are the hollowed parts between the chamfer and the outer circle and the corners of the square. Where two sides of a sunken pocket meet is called a miter. This is a quatrefoil as there are four foils, and most commonly there are also trefoils and cinquefoils.

As seems to be the experience with most geometric creations in wood, there are three inescapable characteristics of tracery that must be followed in order for success to be achieved. Each of these relates to what we will generally describe as the "organized" nature of the work.

1 The design is pure geometry—and all based on the circle, although there was an evolutionary development of the ellipse's being the basis of gothic tracery, somewhere around the 15th century. For now, however, we will stay with the circle.

2 For the best visual appeal, the chamfers all need to be matched so that they are all the same concave curve. This is at least for similar parts of the pattern, and the depths of all the cuts of a similar nature need to be the same, such as for the sunken pockets and the miters.

3 The foils all need to be circles, with flat faces and vertical edges.

10-1. This tracery is from St. Andrew's Cathedral, Inverness, Scotland.

Now, to achieve all this, you will need to embrace the fundamental attitude that everything you do is just as organized.

- ❈ Your drawing and your pattern transfer must be very accurate.
- ❈ Your scroll sawing or fret sawing must be very accurate and executed with sharp blades.
- ❈ Your gouge must not only be very sharp but the bevel must be ground to the right curve for the wood and the pattern.

Steady and well-controlled cuts will achieve a clean, even surface.

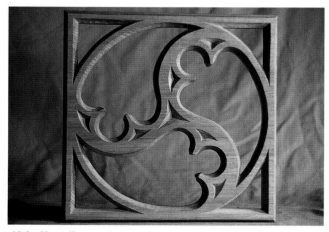

10-2. Clean lines and clean, even gouge work make for smart tracery.

Some Basic Gothic Geometry

We will do the drawing required to achieve 10-2, which was carved in Mountain ash (also known as Tasmanian oak, a generic trade name) dressed to an 11-in (280mm) square, 1⅛ in (30mm) thick. You could also use oak, maple, or mahogany.

There is no point attempting this sort of drawing without a good-quality compass. If the lines don't intersect at the right places, your tracery can never be visually acceptable. Refer now to 10-3. Here is the sequence you can follow to draft your own tracery. You can decide how large to make it by defining for yourself the radius in step one.

1 Define the general size of the trefoil by drawing an outer circle, and draw in the intersecting lines A–B and C–D at 90 degrees to one another.

2 Define the general size of the "window" with the tangents C–A and C–B.

3 Segment the quadrants with the intersecting lines E–E1 and F–F1. As we are producing a trefoil, we need to divide the outer circle into three parts so these intersecting lines are 60 and 30 degrees off A–B and C–D, respectively.

4 Draw in the inner circle, the diameter of which is 50 percent of the distance between the center O and the tangent A–C along the line O–E1. You must measure right to the tangent; do not stop at the circumference of the outer circle.

5 The centers of the trefoils are the intersections X, Y, and Z.

6 Using each of the centers X, Y, and Z, draw in the arcs on which the centers of the foils are located, the radii being equal to 50 percent of the distance X–X1. The point X1 is on the circumference of the outer circle. The two outer foils become the "shoulders" of what might be imaginary angels.

7 Place a perpendicular line at each of X, Y, and Z, on each of the radii O–X1, O–Y1, and O–Z1. These become X–X3, Y–Y3, and Z–Z3. Also draw a 45-degree line on either side of the perpendiculars as shown by X–X2 and X–X4.

8 With a radius X5–X2 and the centers X5, X3, and X6, draw in the arcs that become the angel's head and shoulders. Do the same on the Y-axis and X-axis.

The inside diameters of the actual foils will depend on how thick you want the wood to be between the foils, as well as the angle and size of the chamfer. If you wish to have a flat area between the chamfers, modify your drawing so that it looks like 10-4, which is how the following

10-3. Part of the fun is trying to work out how to draw it.
See if you can draw the tracery in 10-1.

examples were carved. At this stage, you have the final "look" of the trefoil well and truly in your own hands. A chunky cross section may well be the better way to go, as it is not only stronger but is more in keeping with the style of the gothic times from whence it came.

The outside edge of the tail of the trefoil follows the circumference of the circle radius O–X1, and the inside edge sweeps down as shown to meet it. The end of the tail is where it meets the radius that is at 90 degrees to the radius that passes through the centers of the right and left foils of each "angel."

Your drawing should be preserved and a copy used for the workshop activity. You could glue a copy onto the surface of the wood, which is probably a lot easier than trying to trace it on; however, there are some traps with this as you will see shortly.

Wood and Tool Preparation

Before we proceed further, we must discuss the wood and gouge preparation that is appropriate for this carving.

As with all carving, it is important that the tools be in tune with the wood being worked. This doesn't mean major changes each time you set about to do some carving, unless perhaps you want to switch from softer woods to substantially harder ones. However, if you wish to do a reasonable amount of tracery, you may find it best to choose all the tools—a couple of gouges and a skew—and grind their bevel shapes so that they are in perfect harmony with the wood you will be using.

Each of the carvings is of a species known colloquially in Australia as Tasmanian oak, a generic trade name for two main species, Tasmanian messmate and mountain ash, in the same way Pacific maple is really usually one of three varieties of Philippine meranti. Tasmanian oak is not a particularly good carving wood, being sometimes brittle and stringy, and it can be quite dense. It is similar in some ways to American white oak, although it is finer; but it must not be confused with English or European oak, which cuts much more crisply and cleanly—these are not as "tough."

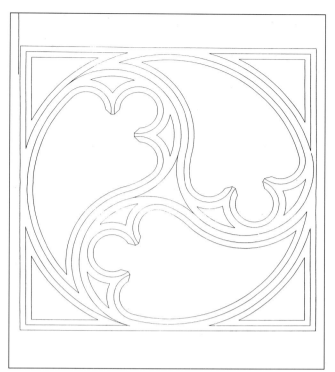

10-4. Add to your drawing the lines for the chamfers.

The gouge shown in 10-5, 10-6, and 10-7 is the one that was used for the curved concave chamfers. It is perfect in bevel shape for the piece of wood and the person who carved 10-2 such that in one controlled sweep each of the foils was cut spontaneously, with a naturally clean surface. You could also use a short bent tool, which for some people will be easier.

10-5. This is the bevel angle used to carve 10-2. It is in perfect harmony with the wood and the carver.

10-6. Notice the shiny spots on the same gouge? These are blunt spots that must be polished off, so that one-sweep cutting can occur.

10-7. This is a pleasant curve for chamfers in tracery. Too deep is too difficult to get smooth, and too flat does not make enough shadow.

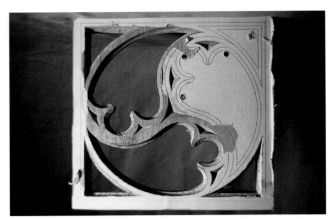

10-8. *If the pattern is not glued on properly, you could end up with it severely damaged during the hole drilling (to accommodate the scroll saw or coping saw blade) or the scroll sawing or carving processes.*

10-9. *A blunt blade and poor proficiency with a scroll saw is not a happy combination for this work. The jagged edges in this foil and the poor tool work combine to make a sad picture.*

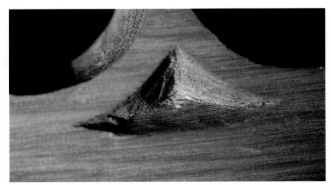

10-10. *This close view of the pocket shows what happens when a skew that is too small and blunt is used. A ⁵⁄₁₆-in (8mm) tool was used, when a ¾-in (20mm) tool is ideal. With practice a small pocket can be created with three cuts.*

The preparation of tracery for carving requires the use of a scroll saw (or coping saw if you don't have access to one), so you will need to be sure the wood you intend to use is not too difficult to process in this manner. You must also ensure the blade is sharp—a blunt blade will burn the wood (if you are using a scroll saw) and most likely will not cut vertically (it will cut in a curved or bowed shape). If you are not proficient with the saw you use for the piercing, you may also end up with a rough, serrated cut instead of a smooth one. If you glue your pattern on, be careful that it is glued securely so that in the sawing process it doesn't get damaged as in 10-8.

In 10-9 you can see the results of both a blunt blade and poor proficiency with the scroll saw, particularly in the bottom right-hand corner and around the tail of the foil. You can clearly see the jagged edge.

In 10-10 is the detail of a poorly executed surface in a sunken pocket. This was done with a skew, which was too small for the task. An 8mm tool was used instead of a size around ¾ in (20mm). Very often as your skill level grows, you will find yourself gravitating towards larger rather than smaller sizes. Your tool control will be such that working with larger tools will become easier and easier, and the speed with which you execute your work will increase. You will also be able to avoid more easily situations like the damage in this sunken pocket. An example of many things going badly can be seen in 10-11.

10-11. *Both poor scroll saw and tool work are visible here. Notice the furry specks all over the edges of the pockets and the chamfers? This is because the wood was not cut cleanly, and it was oiled before it was cleaned up, raising all the partly cut fibers.*

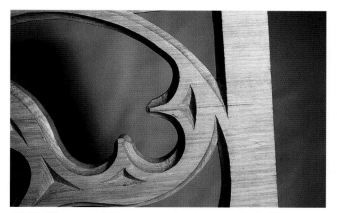

10-12. The successful tracery carving is symmetrical. Different-sized cusps and chamfers like these are not part of the formula.

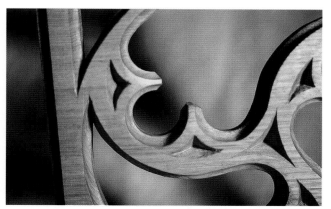

10-13. What a difference when everything is in equilibrium!

A fairly good piece of work is shown in 10-12 that is spoiled by details such as the cusps' being of different widths and the uneven sweep in the curves, particularly on the top right-hand shoulder. This is the result of poor scroll saw work that has been sanded to partially correct it, instead of being adjusted with a fine file or a very carefully controlled, very sharp gouge. An illustration that shows the difference uniformity makes can be seen in 10-13.

Vises and Mallets

Special care must be taken when holding this carving on the workbench. If you look back at 10-8 and examine carefully the "head" foil on the left-hand side, you will see a jagged part interrupting the chamfer. It has in fact been broken and re-glued, although not completely back in the right place. It was damaged because it was clamped too tightly without support underneath in a vise that gripped it along the edges at the top and bottom illustration and squeezed—fracturing the wood at the weak point of the foil. A much safer method of holding this carving is to use the pegboard style of device.

Using a mallet on this carving may similarly make it susceptible to fracturing, so this must be done very carefully; this must be another consideration when choosing the wood you might use for tracery. Brittle wood that easily breaks under stress where there is a small cross section (as Tasmanian oak does) is not the ideal choice. However, if you can master it, then you will add another level to your "skill bank." We discussed in Chapter 3, though, that given the right conditions, any-thing can be carved, so 10-14 shows another example of an excellent execution of this pattern in difficult Tasmanian oak.

Once the carving is completed, and the perimeters of the sweeps and pockets are clean and even, a well-sharpened scraper or a firm sanding block with a fine (say, 400-grit) paper can be used to clean up the face for a keen presentation. If you do use a scraper for this kind of work, be very careful that you hold it flat to the surface, because the widths of the remaining wood are quite narrow and a scraper at an angle will cause tear-out on the corners. Similarly, a soft, pliable block with abrasive paper will also cause damage—by rounding off the sharp edges that you are trying to create. Rounded edges will dull the overall look and remove the crispness from the shadows.

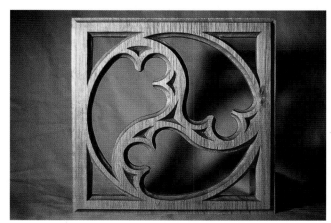

10-14. Sand or scrape the face clean and flat. If the chamfers and pockets are neatly cut, a good result should be achieved.

MEDIEVAL MONSTERS

A Misere Seat

In A.D. 1255, England saw its first elephant. It came from Africa, and was a gift from King Louis IX of France to King Henry III of England. An unknown woodcarver celebrated the arrival of this monster from across the seas by carving what is known as a misere seat, today on display in the Cathedral Church of Saint Peter in Exeter in southern England. A misere seat is a hinged seat that one could rest against when it was in the "up" position if one had to stand for prolonged periods during a church service; one could sit on it when it was in the "down" position.

A tourist's snapshot of the seat taken in April 1994 is seen in 11-1.

Medieval design is quite distinguishable by its crude nature. Sometimes grotesque and ugly, it was also very commonly humorous, at least to the person who did the design. The "Exeter Elephant," as it has become known in ecclesiastical circles, is no exception, although whether the errors in the design of the elephant are intended humor or innocent mistakes is impossible to know. The extract on the following page, is an interesting summary of the carving:

Matthew Paris was an historian of the time, and the "sinister" is the right side from the observer's point of view and the dexter the left—this is terminology commonly used when discussing heraldry."

There are many misericords still in existence in medieval churches, many depicting different aspects of everyday life of the period. In this chapter we will examine the challenges associated with carving our interpretation of a copy of the photograph shown below of the Exeter Elephant. It's not quite like having the real thing on our workbench!

Interpreting the Photograph

The first challenge is to determine how big we are going to make our elephant seat. From the photograph, we have absolutely no idea of its dimensions—there is nothing to reference for scale. Our study of different photographs tells us that they are of different sizes—there was no "standard."

"The tusks turn up instead of down, and that the legs, instead of knees have hocks like a horse . . . Otherwise the representation is so accurate that it must have been taken from life . . . indeed the species can be determined; an African elephant. Now Matthew Paris says that the first time an elephant was seen in England was in 1255, It follows that this particular Misericord cannot be earlier than the year 1255. The sinister supporter of the Exeter elephant is the head of a citizen with close-cropped hair; on the dexter is the head of a lady of wealth."

Francis Bond, 1910
Woodcarvings in English Churches, Vol. I, *Misericords*

11-1. It is very important not to try to correct what look like mistakes in medieval design—they are part of the art form.

Here are two additional examples, 11-2 from Chester Cathedral in middle England, and 11-3 the Verger's misere seat in Winchester Cathedral in southern England:

The example from Chester Cathedral is clearly quite deep, and the one from Winchester shows a comparatively much smaller design, with a very curved platform for the seat. You can also see the very rough woodwork under the seat. So how big is our elephant seat? It must have been big enough for a (medieval) bottom to lean on, so 15¾ in (400mm) is reasonable. If we agree on that, then 6 in (150mm) high makes a nice proportion, and it is almost the same as the proportions in our photograph. Let's adopt this for our carving. But how thick is the piece of wood? Thick enough to make a reasonable ledge to lean on, but unfortunately we can't make it any thicker than the wood that we have readily available. In this case, we will carve from kalantis, from the Philippines, and we can only get it a maximum 4 in (100mm) thick, so that is it! In any case, the proportions are all acceptable. Let us proceed with these measurements, and see what we come up against next.

We can see the framing in the lighter-colored wood around the misere in 11-1, which also shows the neck of the lady's head cut through. We can only assume that the other end is the same, for the sake of symmetry. It is reasonable to make this decision and carve it as such. We could decide to carve the necks complete; however, we will proceed with them truncated, pretending that our make-believe client wants our carving exactly as shown in the photograph. We won't invent any more than we already have. We will need to decide the thickness of the back of the seat and the faces at each end and the elephant itself. We also need to decide the angle between the back of the seat and the platform—is it 90 degrees, or less? So many unknowns—each needing a reasonably intelligent resolution if we are to come up with a plausible carving.

11-2. From Chester Cathedral, this more elaborate misere seat is typical of designs that tell stories from ancient times.

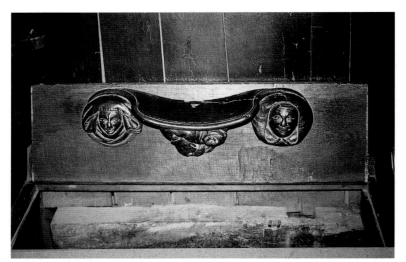

11-3. A very comfortable-looking version from Winchester Cathedral in England. Crude carpentry is visible above and below the seat.

As for the thickness of the back of the seat, obviously it wouldn't be too thin, or it wouldn't survive for long. Certainly not 700 years. So 1³⁄₁₆ in (30mm) is reasonable, and fairly chunky in line with the overall style. We will settle on that. And the angle between the back of the seat and the top of the seat itself? The Chester Cathedral tells us that it is quite reasonable to have one, and the Winchester example tells us that the seat back may actually slope backwards and lean against the wall or paneling behind it. That seems a reasonable proposition, otherwise the seat might fall into the "down" position; so we will angle ours backwards.

Therefore, we need to assume an angle for this. Not too big, not too little—say, 25 degrees off vertical? OK. This means that when the seat part is horizontal to the ground, the back of the seat will be leaning at 25 degrees (see 11-4).

We now have the "mechanics" sorted out as far as we can, given what information we have. So, to the carving itself:

In the illustration we have been given, one thing that is very much missing is any information on the depth of the carving. The photograph has also been taken with a flashlight—you can see the glare on the Plexiglas case the exhibit is in and the shine on the carved surface. What the flash has done is remove shadows that might have given us more detail of the decorations on the surface of the elephant; it has reduced some of the "depth of field" that might have given us clues to the depth of the carving.

A reasonable start is to decide that the "seat" part of the misere will be the full 4 in (100mm) front to back. It is unlikely the elephant would come to the edge of the seat, so we will start it below the level of the front. We need to give a good thickness to the body of the elephant, so let's work on the highest part of the elephant, ³⁄₁₆ in (5mm) below the edge of the seat, the elephant being 1³⁄₁₆ in (30mm) thick, and this will leave 1³⁄₁₆ in (30mm) for the thickness of the seat back. The two heads at the dexter and sinister we will make about half the thickness of the elephant. This should give us enough depth to make a reasonable job of them.

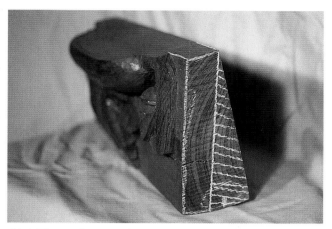

11-4. The carving was hidden from view when the seat was lowered. When raised, the ledge that formed was a convenient resting place if there was a requirement to stand for long periods of time. Here you can see the cross section of the block. The wood to the right of the line will be cut off.

Roughing Out

The first step is the usual one: Mark out the general pattern and begin the roughing out per 11-5.

The removal of large amounts of background requires special thought. It isn't at all difficult, but it can't just be simply attacked in the expectation that everything will survive intact. The temptation is to take out large amounts at a time. Now, this might be perfectly safe to do; however, it is essential that you experiment first. Start with smaller and gradually move

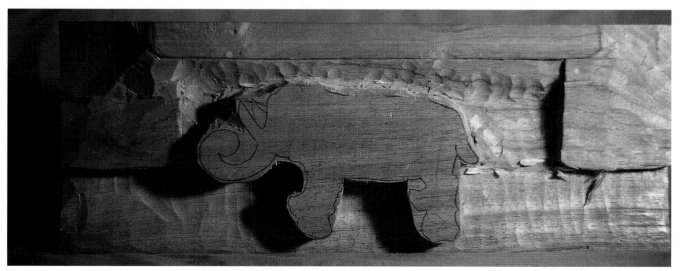

11-5. Plan your roughing out carefully. Some woods split badly if there is an attempt to remove too much waste at once.

11-6. This ear is quite wrong. The medieval version might not be anatomically correct; however, it has an artistic character that this childlike version does not have.

11-7. This elephant is taking on a much better form. The ear is positioned better, and certainly the shape is closer to the original.

towards larger, more vigorous waste removal. The tools you can try for mass removal would be the usual ¾-in (20mm) work horse, and you should also try the 1³⁄₁₆-in (30mm) long, bent flat gouge for more vigorous waste removal. You will of course need your mallet in this situation, more for power than control.

If your wood is prone to splitting, be wary about large bits of waste removal. You may end up with considerable damage if you dig in too deep. It is also essential that you observe the rule of not moving your tool up and down as you would the handle of a tire jack. If you are digging in deep, you run the very real risk of breaking your gouge if you do not let it out of the wood by either pulling it out vertically or letting it fall sideways. Make every cut a clean cut, and don't remove waste by breaking the wood. Recut an incision if necessary.

With larger removal like this, there is a tendency to overlook or forget just where the background is. We get carried away with the removal and start to get a liking for the larger tools, and next thing we have started to dig into what should be the background and we end up damaging it. Once you begin to get close to the background level, it is important that a depth gauge is in constant use. You will also find that at this stage of the removal process, long, bent tools are the best, assisted by smaller tools to get in around the patterns. You are also advised to switch back to the smaller tools if you are in any doubt.

11-8. As the roughing-out phase comes to completion, it is important to establish the final surface of the background. Use a depth gouge frequently, and smooth off the background before carving the faces.

An easy error to make—the wrong ear shape—is shown in 11-6. The photograph of the original has a very definite four-sided ear. The shape in 11-6 is very much a flat top with a curved drop below. It is these kinds of mistake that will cause the carving to come to grief, because the ear is a significant focal point of the work, and if it is not a reasonable likeness it will be very obvious. A much better version, both for positioning and shape, is seen in 11-7.

In 11-8, 11-9, and 11-10 we see the roughing-in in better detail. Note in 11-10 the unfortunate gash along the cheek on the face at the sinister—a rather coincidentally apt name for this misfortune! This is what is known as an "internal check"—not visible from the outside when carving commenced, but sure enough there on the inside. Often this is an unhappy surprise for a carver. Below the neck, and right at the end is another (external) check: the wood is opening up quite badly. It is visible as a long black blur in the bottom right of 11-10. This (the external check) is possibly a result of either one of two things: a change in the moisture content of the wood or a release of stresses that were naturally in the wood before it was cut. The moisture content of the board that this piece was cut from was generally 14 percent, so it is probably to be the latter. The piece was cut from a board 12¼ in × 4 in × 48 in (310mm × 100mm × 1800mm). The internal check in this example most likely originated from a large sap pocket. Significant sized sap veins are not uncommon in this species.

11-9. Pencil in the key parts of the face, starting with the eyes and the nose.

11-10. The internal check that has been exposed could be filled to help hide it, or left for effect.

Carving Faces

It is said that to carve a bust is the hardest subject one will ever do. Whether true or not is largely up to the attitude and inclinations of the carver—suffice it to say that the face carving in this example is not especially demanding, although there are some pointers that if followed will significantly ease the degree of difficulty. Here is a list of the most common mistakes we make when carving a head or face:

- We place the eyes too high into the forehead.
- We overlook the fact that the nose is the most forward part of the face, and we make the face "flat."
- We make the corner of the eye where it meets the nose too shallow—it is actually quite deep at this place.
- We make the mouth too flat—the corners of the mouth should be pushed back towards the ear.
- We forget that the nose is about the same length as the ear and roughly in line with the top and bottom of it.

11-11. Faces often present a seemingly insurmountable set of problems. This need not be so if observation techniques are developed and patiently applied to the work.

11-12. If you get the proportions correct, and the various parts of the face in the right place, then at least you have a chance of creating a reasonable carving.

If you look at 11-11, you will find all of these ingredients, plus another—there are no eyeballs in the sockets. Strangely, despite all the copying and learning of observation techniques, the above list is a very common set of failings for the first time around. So if yours looks like the one in 11-11, you are probably perfectly normal! The person who did this one is! Perhaps the thought of "doing a face" is a bit overwhelming, and so we get thrown off the track of logic and observation a little too easily. 11-12 is a much more satisfactory exhibit.

Now, do you remember the things we said about 11-1's lacking depth of field and the assumptions we made about the depths to which we would carve the various components? Then take a look at 11-13, especially at the faces.

While the faces aren't all that exciting from an artistic point of view, and, ignoring the background removal that isn't complete around the sinister (the carver changed his mind and decided to make the face smaller) the depth of them looks acceptable. Agree? If so, then look at 11-14.

Here we see a perfect example of just how misleading photography can be, and how incredibly careful we need to be when using it as our input. This carver did not follow the assumptions at the end of the section "Interpreting the Photograph," where the depth of the heads was decided at about ⅝ in (15mm). The ones in 11-14 are about ¼ in (6mm). They look reasonable from the front when reproduced as a photograph, but in reality are quite thin and very, very wrong.

11-13. To the inexperienced eye, depth can be difficult to assess, and the viewer can certainly be tricked. Look at these faces, then look at 11-14.

This carver attempted to reproduce the photograph, but did not first correctly interpret the photograph and place the subject back into reality. The photograph has little depth of field, and this is what the carver created. This is quite a trap for the unwary.

There are some other things too. 11-15 is really another very good example. Notice how the carver has interpreted the shine and shadow along the edge of the seat—by a set of two grooves—whereas it really is a convex surface with the camera flash shining on the rounded portion just below the rim.

11-14. The carver has created literally what he thought he saw—and as a result, the faces are so thin (in depth) as to be completely at odds with the original.

11-15. Notice the finger groove along the edge of the seat? The carver has incorrectly interpreted the shine and shadow in 11-1.

the hooves of a cow. These miserere seats mostly date from the late 13th-century. They lift up to support a standing man.

by the
Chapel
cloisters
toration
to the
Exeter.
and muc
cathedral
Lady C
again us

Page 14

11-16. New information, a new perspective, and we can reassess some of our original assumptions.

11-17, 11-18, 11-19. A new seat shape, a new face, and an altered ear are just some of the changes resulting from the new information. The carver, whose incorrect interpretation resulted in 11-13 and 11-14, did a completely new carving after finding the additional photograph shown in 11-16 and reinterpreting what he saw. The revised version is in 11-20.

There is something else, though, that is even more puzzling about this carving: The "mistakes" we have talked about so far are all typical of how we might do our first exercise like this. Except that in 11-13, do you notice that the "necks" are not truncated as we said we would do in the very beginning, and that there appears to be a border carved in relief around the ends and bottom of the elephant? So, what is going on?

Quite simply, it turns out, the carver was using a different photograph from the one we set out to use, so this person had a different slant on things. 11-16 is that photograph, reproduced by courtesy of the Very Reverend Keith Jones, Dean of St. Peter's Cathedral of Exeter in England, and it shows a quite different view. The photograph is a reproduction from a 1968 information booklet by the Very Reverend Marcus Knight. This gives us some completely new information to assess, and here are some of the observations we can make:

※ The assumption about the angle of the seat to the back seems about right.
※ The assumption about the relationship of the depth of the elephant to the depth of the seat is about right, although the seat looks to be deeper than the 4 in (100mm) we have allowed.
※ We can see more clearly the depth and detail of the faces.

Look at the elephant's ear—the shadow in the corner at the top where it is connected to the head. This is a considerably different shape from that in 11-7. It is clues such as these that make all the difference to the end work.

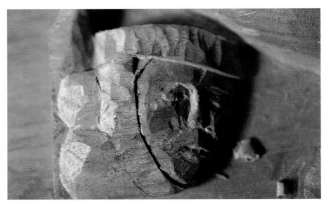

11-18

11-19

And the border carved in 11-5? What it actually is, is the impression made over hundreds of years of the seat resting on its supporting framework when it was in the "down" position. The carver of 11-5 interpreted the shadow the wrong way, and carved it as a raised border, when in fact it is a compressed border. This is another depth-of-field problem—where an impression can indeed look like the opposite, the image playing tricks on the eye. We can now also see why the necks are truncated at the sides—because the original A.D. 1255 carving was too wide for the seat frame it sat on (whether then or at some later time) and the necks were modified to allow it to fit.

There certainly aren't any "finger grips" in the edge around the top of the seat. Interestingly, the carver of the unfinished work in 11-15 made a similar mistake, carving two grooves.

The roundness of the seat appears to be greater than in the assumptions we have made. This is most likely because the seat is deeper than we assumed (100mm). Now, this could change the "look" significantly, so we should examine this more closely. If we modify our carving to take in this new information, 11-17 shows a reasonable new pattern. The solid-white area represents the additional waste that now needs to be removed to better approximate the curve of the seat in the new photographic input.

Note the rather messy knot right in the center of the seat in 11-17 and the wavy grain on either side of it. It is this piece that has the internal check on the sinister face and the splitting occurring at the end also near the face. Altogether not a very nice piece of wood.

More detail of the dexter face in progress is shown in 11-18. The angle of the carving (the general plane of the face) in relation to the background is greater than it might otherwise have been; this is also a result of the additional input. It is unclear from the original color photograph that the angle would be this great. Study the different information "takeout" from these photographs carefully—they really do tell quite different stories.

The ear revised to take into consideration the new shadow information is shown in 11-19. This is an excellent example of the use of lighting for shadow. In this case, the shadow information was so poor that the ear was being carved quite incorrectly. And what a difference it makes to have it right.

If you do take photographs as reference material for future carving, whatever you do make absolutely sure the shapes you need to know are properly recorded. You may need to supplement your photographs with sketches, measurements, or written notes. You may have noticed that nearly all the photographs in this book are lit from one side or the other. That is so shadows will be created that help indicate shape and relative size.

11-20. A creditable second effort, although the border incorrectly remains in relief. The interpretation of depth is much more in line with the original. The wood in this example is white meranti, finished in gold shellac.

11-21, 11-22. In Chapter 6 we also looked at copying someone else's work. It is particularly difficult to capture character and style. The finish on these carvings is walnut oil, a traditional medieval surface treatment.

11-22

11-20 is the second effort by the same carver who produced the too-thin faces in 11-14. Note, however, the border is still raised instead of compressed. Two additional examples are shown in 11-21 and 11-22. You might like to make your own critique, based on 11-1 and 11-16.

chapter 12

SHADOWY LIES

A Jacobean Cartouche

A cupboard door or a pediment on a sideboard will, of necessity, mostly be carved without much depth to the pattern. The thickness of the wood will not allow it. How, then, do we give ourselves visual depth when it doesn't exist at all? How can we offer richness when there just doesn't seem enough wood to do it? We simply have to tell some lies! We need to know how to make things look like they aren't, make something look round when it is almost flat. We need to be able to create illusion.

In Chapter 1 we started a discussion about shadows. We began to see that the shadow is the carver's paint pot. Light, dark, and everything in between. We saw in Chapter 5 how shadows can interfere with our drawing. We considered shadow in Chapter 7 from the point of view of its impact on our carving. We saw the need for crispness of the curve on the leaf when light shines across it and the undercut that increases the visual strength of the artwork by "lifting" it from the background. Light, and dark. The carver's paint pot.

But now, it is time to move into another dimension. Shadowy lies? Yes, that just about sums it up. We will see that we can play tricks, and make things look like they aren't. Something round that's almost flat? Something thick that's so very thin?

Something far away that's very close? Something that looks the opposite of what it actually is? Telling lies? You bet!

First, let's really understand what shadows do.

Take a look out your window. Into the garden, at the building next door, down the street. It doesn't matter. When you do, though, take time to really study what you are looking at. It's best if it is a sunny day. If it is cloudy, things will be duller, but they will still be there. What things? These things called shadows. And if the clouda are coming and going so the shadows are changing, that is even better, so that you can see the differences between some shadow and no shadow on the same object.

What shadow does is create illusion. It increases or decreases space (distance) perception. If shadow on an object is graduated (in intensity, meaning strong or week or in between), it goes a step further and alters our perception of its shape. So, alterations in the nature of the shadow on and/or surrounding a subject can alter our perception of its closeness and its shape.

Perhaps you are looking out your window and you see a large wall on a house painted a light cream color. The sun is shining on this wall at an angle so that the rainwater drainpipe on the wall has a shadow on one side and not the other. Where the shadow is falling down the side of the drainpipe the depth perception is altered and the wall might actually look as though it is "stepped" in along that line. Or, have you ever seen the effect of a screen door when it is closed, together with the main door, and there is light shining on the screen? The screen casts a shadow over the closed door, and makes it look as if there is no door there at all and that you are looking into the inside of a dark room. Go for a walk down your street and see if you can find this or the drainpipe effect, or something similar.

If you refer to illustrations 11-13 and 11-15 on page 117 in Chapter 11, "Medieval Monsters," you will see the misinterpretation of shine and shadow by two carvers looking at a photograph of a misere seat. They carved "finger" grooves along the front top of the seat when in fact they weren't there at all in the original, because it was their perception—the original photograph indicated hollows both depth and shape illusion.

The creation of illusion by shadow is a skill that can really only be learned by observation and practice. You must see for yourself what a slight change of surface shape or an undercut here or there will do to the

12-1. Playing card designs offer many design opportunities for relief carving.

appearance of the work. Set yourself up with a good cross light—but not so strong that it is too bright and becomes irritating—and start to experiment with alterations to the shape of a curved surface. Make it flatter. Give it an acutely curved edge. Undercut it. And as you do these things, stand back and see just what effects you are creating.

To understand illusion, it is easier to start with a finished carving and see what was done rather than to work through it from the beginning. So, here are two examples of some illusions that are quite fascinating. Once we have looked at them, we will examine an example you could try for yourself:

First, consider 12-1, a carved panel (Honduras mahogany), 35½ in × 3 in × 48 in (900mm × 75mm × 1200mm), of the Knave of Spades from the Swiss playing card set "The Alchemists," designed in 1700.

The carving is in three planks laminated lengthwise, each plank being roughed out before gluing up. The bucket ropes and the knave's right-hand yoke are completely undercut from the background by some 1³⁄₁₆ in (30mm).

The part to consider for this discussion is the village pump stand: the vertical cylindrical member of the pump, and specifically the largest diameter part from and including the base, up towards the hand of the knave.

The graphic shown in 12-2, which is aligned with the carving, represents the cross section of the pedestal of the pump. The concave curve in the graphic represents that part of the pedestal that is the top of the base, that looks like it is level witho the ground in the carving. The way the carving is lit by the prevailing lighting (which is coming from the viewer's left) makes this concave surface, which is protruding no further than the maximum 3-in

(75mm) thickness of the planks, look much further out towards the viewer. The edge of this base is cut so that it slopes back in towards the background and then is undercut to the background level. This sloping backwards alters the lighting (increases the shadow) across this surface relative to the concave one, and makes it look vertical in relation to it, when in fact they are both, in reality, almost on the same plane—about ¼-in (6mm) difference—and in conflict with the impression they give.

Complicated? Yes, but logical. Take the base of the village pump, for instance. If you want something that is almost vertical (the top of the base) to look as if it might be horizontal, you need to bounce reflected light in a more upward direction than in a downward one. The only way to do this is to make the surface like a concave mirror that will reflect light towards its theoretical spherical center—that is, outwards and in this case in a direction upwards. This tends to

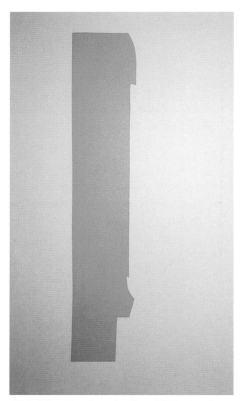

12-2. The direction of reflected light may have a major impact on the appearance of shapes, and may make them look quite different from the truth.

12-3. Shadows create the illusion of greater depth in this 10mm deep carving, "The Terrace." (Courtesy of Mr. Andrew Tarlington)

make it look as though it might be coming at you more than sloping to the ground. The reason for having the edge of the base sloping back in towards the background is to compensate for the upward and outward look of the concave surface. The shadow on it recesses it (pushes it backwards) so that you have the top facing out and up and the bottom facing out and down, and together you tend to get the impression that the top is horizontal and the edge is vertical. Obviously this is not perfect and the visual result is not exactly horizontal and vertical, but it is much more so than it might have been otherwise. Lies with light!

In the next example, there are some more clever shadowy lies.

The carving in 12-3 is from jelutong framed with meranti stained a dark color. The stair rails and posts are made as separate components and glued on. The jelutong is 1 in (25mm) thick, and the maximum depth of any of the carving is ⅜ in (10mm)—original surface to back wall. From the front of the lounge to the front of the back cushions is ³⁄₁₆ in (5mm).

Notice how the wide shadow around the cutaway from your left of the lounge (up and across where the ceiling would be) gives the impression of depth, with the staircase disappearing up into it. We immediately get a mental image of a room deep enough for a stairwell. The curtains on our right, carved on the angled wall, have the folds undercut so that any side light will be caught and will create the impression of a folded curtain. The shadows on the stair treads and underneath their edges make them look wider and almost horizontal, when in fact they are almost vertical. The shadows between the bottom and the back cushions on the lounge make them look deep and comfortable. Shadowy lies!

Carving Rolled Scrolls

We move on now, then, to a seemingly simple exercise that will surely get you thinking!

We will examine the carving of a Jacobean-style cartouche, in black bean. A cartouche (from the French) is a scroll-like ornament. We will analyze the finished product, relating it back to a simple line drawing. What we are going to do is understand why the carver did what he/she did, within the parameters that were set. The following discussion relates to 12-4 and 12-5 unless otherwise stated.

12-4. Dress your wood to 6 in × 1 in × 13¾ in (150mm × 25mm × 350mm). We used black bean; you could also use padauk, yew, or teak.

12-5. The roundness of the scrolls is enhanced by dishing the flatter parts of the scroll.

Understanding What the Carver Did

We are examining the carving of a Jacobean-style cartouche that is shown on the previous page in 12-5, relating it back to the simple line drawing shown in 12-4. In analyzing the finished product, we are trying to understand why the carver did what he/she did, within the parameters that were set. The parameters are:

✳ A reasonably dark wood—this means that for the shadows to stand out, they will need to be very well executed. Weaker, softer shadows will not be as effective on darker wood as they might be on a lighter color.

✳ A very shallow depth of carving—maximum 5mm, as indicated in 12-6. This means that there will need to be some skillful curves created to make things look round when they aren't too round at all.

12-6. The depth of the carving is no more than ⅜ in (5mm).

With the exception of the incised "spears" radiating from each corner, the carving of the scroll will not go below the level of the background surface. This means that we can't crib any extra depth by carving any deeper anywhere more than 5mm from the original surface. The center of the bead in the rosette should be approximately the same height as the topmost part of each scroll.

✳ Surface finish—low sheen. This means that there will be a lower level of light reflection so that those surfaces will not be too shiny. This will help the strength of the shadows because light will not be reflected so much from one surface to another and cause a weakening of shadows, particularly undercuts, which are designed to create darkness.

First, you will notice that the carving is not a perfect match of the drawing. The carver has taken some license and put some "personal" touches to the design. This is a perfectly normal attribute. Later we will also see three more versions of this design. Unless there is a specific requirement for an exact rendition, any artist will want to make little changes that he/she thinks might look better.

The design can be easily broken down into its components: four scrolls, with a center rosette and strapping. The straps are the flat strips that radiate from the rosette and appear to pierce the rolled portion of the scrolls.

The rosette is relatively simple to carve, and we won't dwell on it. It is easier than the Tudor rose discussed in Chapter 5.

Once the pattern is transferred to the wood, the first thing to do is to remove the background to the 5mm level. The best tool for leveling the background is a fairly flat, wide, long bent gouge. Once this is done, you have a clear run at the pattern.

The first priority is to create the impression of roundness in the rolled-up parts of the scroll. There isn't much room (depth), so we need to draw on all the illusory tricks we can. The first of these is to realize that the eye doesn't just see the rolled scroll, it sees the whole of the carving at the one time. To assist in the illusion of roundness, if we make the whole thing look curved, then we have done a lot to succeed in our mission. Therefore, if we make the flat part of the

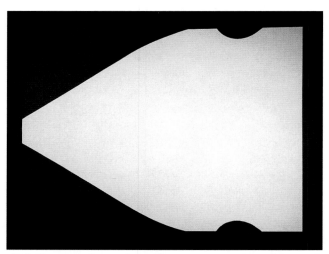

12-7. Use a template such as this to create a mockup of the scroll, which will make it easier to understand its structure.

scroll (from the rosette to the rolled part) curved, then we have successfully begun our lie-telling. The flat parts are themselves dished with the areas nearest the rosette, the shallowest and the areas nearest the rolled parts the deepest. Thus we immediately get the impression that the "paper" is curled from the center outwards to the rolled end. Don't forget to leave in the strapping—it's actually easy to cut it off without realizing before it is too late. It too should follow the same contour as the scroll. If it is too thick and doesn't follow this contour, it will look cumbersome and out of place. The end of the strap that protrudes beyond the rolled part is turned upwards a little by sloping it down towards the bottom of the rolled edge. It is important that it also look like it is a continuation of the strap on the inside, so you need to get the bottom of that cut equal in depth to the top of the strap on the inside of the roll.

Once you have the strapping in place and the dishing done, you will have exposed the part that you need to turn into a roll. There are two key elements to the creation of the roll. First, you will need to study the actual structure of the roll. The scroll as designed is a somewhat distorted example, and it is easy to "misunderstand" it. The easiest way to come to grips with it is to make a paper template from the pattern in 12-7. Draw it on a sheet of 8½-in × 11-in paper and roll it up, and you will see the structure of the roll. Roll your piece of paper from the wide end until you have replicated the carving.

Depending on the size of your carving, you will need one or two quite small tools to clear the waste from the ends of the roll. The remainder is done with a sharp skew chisel. It is very important that the skew work produce an evenly curved and smooth surface. Don't forget, you can use your skew as a scraper to clean off facets. If a smooth and evenly curved surface is not achieved, it is not possible to create the desired effect of the roll. The "trick" to the shape of the surface of the roll is simple. The edges should be very round, while the top should be barely curved but certainly not flat. 12-8 shows a scroll that is a little on the flat side. The edges of the scroll are not round enough, and this makes the top look flat, in spite of

12-8. Make the left and right edges rounder to make the top look less flat.

the fact that it cannot, given the depth of the carving, be made much rounder. It is the round edge that visually "squeezes" the top surface upwards and makes it look rounder. 12-9 has a rounder look to it, but notice how the light is catching along a facet on the right-hand edge, spoiling the round look of the top. Because of this "demarcation line" the top looks flat. This is why it is important to have an even (unbroken) curved surface. A simple scrape along this facet with the skew would remove this ridgelike line.

12-9. Clean off the facets on the round surfaces—scrape them or use fine steel wool, which has a cutting, rather than an abrading, action.

12-10. *If the background had been completely removed, the overall effect would have been to make the carving look deeper. The carver has produced a fine rosette, choosing simplicity for a clutter-free design.*

12-11. *Nonparallel sides spoil the effect of the scroll.*

The overall effect of this cartouche is shown in 12-10. (Note how the scrolls are not as round-looking as in 12-15.) The fact that the background has not been entirely removed also tends to place too broad a shadow around the cartouche, tending to detract from the pattern itself and weakening it a little. As a result of the flatter carving, the shadows are not as strong as they could be either. (Note that 12-5, 12-10, and 12-12 are lit identically, so you can easily compare the shadow intensity as a result of the final shape and degree of undercutting.)

A nicely executed roll is shown in 12-11, except that the sides are not straight and parallel the full length of the roll on the inside edge. The ends have been rounded slightly on the corners, and this tends to reduce the definition of the scroll. Compare it with 12-12, which has straight and parallel edges and no square-edged facets on the surface to interfere with the rolled-up look.

12-13 shows for the most part a pleasing and spontaneous form. The scrolls aren't all of the same "tightness"—compare the left-hand end scroll to the right-hand end—but it doesn't seem to

12-12. *Parallel sides make the scroll more realistic, and stronger shadows make it look rounder.*

12-13. *This is a spontaneous carving that would have been improved with a higher standard of finish.*

matter with this carving. One of the characteristics of black bean, however, is that it tends to break away on fine edges. It will chip easily if the tool is not very sharp. Black bean is also a waxy wood, and if the tool is sharp it will polish itself as you carve it. Notice the chip on one of the petals on the rosette, and around various parts of the perimeter of the scrolls.

Do you also notice the dust in 12-13? It is in 12-14 as well. This is because we oiled (almond oil in these cases) the carvings without their being perfectly clean, and the dust stuck to the surface.

This scroll in 12-14 is very worth looking at. The rolled parts are not too dissimilar from those in 12-13, with regard to their "openness." The rolls are not too tight, but somewhat larger and looser. As a result the volume of shadow within the ends of the rolls is much greater and this accentuates their presence, because there is a greater mass of contrast. The surfaces of the round parts of the roll are well curved, even if there is a little too much of the skew work showing. Some scraping would remove this immediately.

The end result is a strongly shadowed, very visible set of scrolls, the complete carving seen in 12-15.

12-14. Make sure that all the dust and "furry" surfaces and edges are cleaned off before oiling.

12-15. Strong shadows give good depth illusion, especially to the scrolls.

MIRROR, MIRROR, ON THE WALL . . .

A Mirror Crest

The mirror crest is our first real move towards carving in the round. We will carve in high relief and use shadows for realism as opposed to illusion—carving foliage with crisp, clean edges, smooth-flowing surfaces, and clean, strong shadows. Our pattern includes a traditional scallop shell, and we will compare our carving to a real shell and check how realistic we are. The richness of the carvings on picture and mirror frames introduces us to fancy wall plaques, and it is also our introduction to thinking about things like carving components separately and putting them together. We will do this in Chapter 17.

The pattern in 13-1 is transferred to the wood dressed to 12 in × 2 in × 8¾ in (300mm × 50mm × 220mm) in the usual way, and the outline profile is cut before carving commences. This can be done with a scroll saw, band saw, or more laboriously by hand. If you are using a harder wood and a scroll saw, make sure you start with a fresh blade, and watch that it doesn't need replacing during the cutting process. If it starts to get blunt, it may burn the wood, and may not cut vertically. Make sure the grain is running top to bottom of the pattern—the 12-in (300mm) width runs across the grain. If you intend to attach the crest to a mirror, here are some tips that may make the process proceed a little more smoothly:

Purchase the actual mirror before you start to make the frame. This way, you know you are able to complete the project; you won't discover that you have a beautiful frame and can't, for whatever reason, get the right-sized mirror. You will also know the exact shape to make the frame and crest. It is always a good idea to check that you have all of the "ingredients" together before you start the carving—include the ingredients listed in the side box at the right.

The wood that has been chosen for this project is rose mahogany. It is a typical good-quality furniture wood, a hardwood, with a distinctively pleasant rose perfume. It is relatively easy to work; however, it is brittle along sharp edges, so for carving it is best to have rounded corners and no otherwise thin parts of the design. Its average dry density is approximately 1265 lb/yd³ (720 kg/m³). You could also use alder or totara.

13-1. Be sure to purchase the actual mirror before you start any work. It may be necessary to modify the shape of your plans to suit the mirror that you are able to get.

Preparation

The easiest way to hold the pattern for carving is on a pegboard as in 13-2, so you will need to prepare this as well. The burning from a blunt blade is clearly visible in 13-3. While much of this will be carved away, nevertheless the overheating of the wood may make it more brittle, and the depth of the burn, while most likely only superficial, may interfere with the carving. You will also notice, from 13-3, that the back of the carving has not been rabbeted to take a mirror. The bottom of the carving that has so far been done (on the right-hand end) is where the rabbet should start. Now, it is most undesirable to rabbet after the carving is done. If there is an accident, which is all too easy, then the hours of carving time may well be wasted. As a principle, always prepare the wood completely before doing any decoration. This is essential not only from the accident point of view, but it may also have an influence on your design if you can see the exact shape you have to work—you will not be fooled into carving into something that will be removed. (A rabbeted crest is shown in 13-14.)

The preparation of the wood completely before carving also means you need to thoroughly plan the work. For example, is the crest to be carved on one side or on both (as in the case of a freestanding mirror)? Now, this might seem like a silly question to make sure you ask yourself; however, rest assured that the number of times you will be well into a creative pursuit only to wish you "had thought of that before" will make you mad. So, better up front, don't you think? In this chapter we will review examples that have been carved on both sides.

13-2. Prepare a pegboard sturdy enough to take a lot of mallet work. The pegs should be close-fitting so there is no movement of the carving.

13-3. It is essential to prepare the wood completely, including rabbeting, before you commence carving.

Design and Making

We have talked a lot about interpretation of photographs and drawings. During this and the next two chapters, we are going to discuss making up your own patterns. You will notice in 13-1 that there is no detail on the foliage, only the outline. How do we go about creating the pattern? Let's start by looking at a finished one, in 13-4, and compare it with the drawing:

The Shell

In the drawing there is a border around the scalloped perimeter of the shell. The real scallop shell in 13-5 and 13-6 has no such border—no scallop species do—and the carvers in two of the examples we will review elected to take the "realistic" path, leaving out this design border.

13-4. Compare this carving with the drawing in 13-1. The scroll and shell are quite different. The maker carved the other side as well, which is shown in 13-15.

*13-5, 13-6. This is the scallop **Pecten fumatus** spp., found in the western Pacific and on the east coast of Australia. The shell in the drawing (13-1) is derived from the species **Pecten jacobaeus**, or "St. James" shell, which is used symbolically in heraldry. It comes from the Mediterranean, Cape Verde Islands, and northwest African coast.*

13-7. *This scroll is from a panel in Lanoch Castle in Dunedin, New Zealand. (Courtesy of Mr. Don Mckerrell)*

13-8, 13-9, 13-10. These carvings are all representations of the same line drawing. Each is totally different, but they all fall within the same outside border. None of them represent real botanical species, but all of them are recognizable as "foliage."

The Scroll

In the drawing in 13-1 the scroll has a "window" in the face of it. None of the carvers of the examples shown liked this idea, so they left it out. They decided that to leave it out it was more in keeping with the more "realistic" approach they wanted to take with their design. They preferred the simpler style, like the one in 13-7. Their decision was also influenced by the complexity that they wished to put into the foliage, and they considered that there would be conflict with a scroll that was too "busy."

It is important to note that woodcarving is an art form, and as such the carver has complete freedom to carve whatever he or she likes without offending "convention." We should still be cognizant, though, that sometimes we will be rightly criticized if we vary too much from a historic period style and still pass it off as representing that style. If a "window" in a scroll is a part of convention for a particular region or historic period, then we should be mindful of this so that we describe our work correctly.

The Foliage

The first thing to do before spending too much time on the foliage is to carve away the waste and "expose" the shell. You can leave the detail on the shell for a later time, but at least get it formed ready for decoration before tackling the foliage. It is too difficult, and there is no reason, to plan the foliage until its form is completely exposed by the carving of the shell.

The foliage has two main "ridgelines" in the drawing, as in 13-1. As we have said previously, the form or basic shape of the carving should be developed before the decoration is done, so the shaping of the undulating areas must be done before the foliage decoration itself is carved. The undulating cross section can be seen in 13-3. If you intend to carve the reverse side as well, carve the topside first while the back is still flat and easy to hold on the pegboard, and then do the back. If you plan your carving carefully, you will be able to leave the tip of the shell, the ends of the scroll, and the highest part of the foliage on either side all at the same plane. These will become stable resting points for the front of the crest while you carve the back.

In each of 13-8, 13-9, 13-10, and 13-11 there is a different treatment of the same line drawing. Each follows the general dual-focal ridgelines already mentioned, although 13-11 is in less detail than the others are. The individual leaves tend to come from the bottom perimeter of the carving, which is like a branch, whereas in the others all the leaves tend to flow from the scroll itself. There is no right or wrong; however, the flow from the scroll is more "traditional." Could 13-11, then, be "art nouveau"?

This raises the question of realism. Just how real should we be? Does it matter? How do you decide? We started out in Chapter 5 trying to emulate nature. And now, it seems we are making up things as we go along. So what is right and what is wrong?

13-9

13-10

It depends entirely on your objective. And that is about where it starts and stops. If you are going to create a particular species of leaf, then that is what you should do. Find some samples and photographs, study them, and make your carving accordingly. There is not much point in saying that something is something it isn't.

Having said that, it is important to reconsider what we said in Chapter 5 about recognition. We will use the scallop shell as an example. Whether or not you carve the shell as per the drawing or the shell photograph, so long as you represent the fundamental form of the shell, it will always be recognized as a scallop. There are a great many different varieties of scallop, many that look nothing much like our drawing at all, but these are not recognizable by most people either. The "traditional" scallop shell, like the one in the drawing, was arguably made "famous" through heraldry and carried into different situations like this mirror crest. It has even been used as a logo for a brand of gasoline. And none of the applications use a perfect reproduction of the shell, only a recognizable version of it. 13-11 is a good example.

Here, the carver has in fact carved the shell in a convex shape rather than the concave the others used. The other examples have used the inside of the shell as the motif for the front of the

crest, and this carver has used the outside of the shell as the motif. Logic may well present a strong case that the other carvers are wrong and this one is right! Yet traditionally it is the other way around. Whatever your attitude, the convex carving is nothing like a real one; however, it is still clearly recognizable as a scallop. There is no answer. No one is right or wrong.

13-11. *This shell is carved convex, not concave, and it follows more closely the original drawing. The surface of the shell may have been better left unrealistically flat, rather than try to emulate a natural surface. This crest is being prepared for use as a table ornament. Note that the flow of the foliage on the left side is not the same as on the right.*

13-12. The shell "ribs" are similar to the original drawing. Very pronounced ridgelines at the bottom right- and left-hand corners add strength to the form.

13-13. This is the reverse side of 13-12. A cleaner surface on the shell and clearer definition of the ribs would have improved the carving.

Compare the two executions shown in 13-11 and 13-12. 13-11 is more effective than 13-12, if you use shadow formation as the criteria, but to the traditionalist the latter will be more attractive. Both carvers tried to reproduce the natural "rippled" effect that the surface of a real shell has, both with varying degrees of success. It might have been better to leave the surfaces unrealistically flat. 13-13 is the reverse of 13-12, and essentially follows the original drawing. Notice the addition of the thistle? A nice personal touch. 13-14 shows the full back with the rabbeted area. 13-15 shows the reverse side of 13-3, with some more aquatic life added for effect. The horizontal lines that are across the flutes in the shell are not a part of any species at all, but nevertheless are quite effective. In this photograph, the foliage from the front that wraps around the sides is visible. We will come back to this shortly.

In each of the finished crests discussed here, the carver marked the proposed ridgelines on the wood, shaped the form work, and then drew directly onto the wood the proposed foliage. It is a little impossible to draw on paper first and then transfer to the wood because of the shape of the formed background. The very pronounced ridges in 13-11 make for a striking design. However, the flow of the foliage on the left side is different from that on the right and this detracts from the overall effect. Be careful also that, if everything is so perfect and "clinically" correct, the charm of the handmade piece is not lost as a result.

13-14. Here is a rabbet done to the shape of an existing mirror. It is different from the original pattern.

13-15. *This is the reverse side of 13-4. It has a more natural and tidier feel than the front. For the front, the carver tried to do something with an existing drawing. On the back, he did his own thing for a more relaxed and happier result.*

13-16. *The square look does not work. It is essential to form the curves, then decorate them with the leaves.*

13-17. *Compare the difference when the form is in place, before decorating commences. It looks more natural and is easier to do.*

These are the artistic "balances" that need to be considered as you develop your skills and design ideas. If the carving is to be added to a machined frame, for example, a carving that is too much in the direction of "hand done" may look out of place. If you are in doubt about the degree of finesse needed in the finished carving to give the required degree of balance, then experiment with a small machined section. Place the work on it at regular intervals during its development to help you with this assessment process.

As we said earlier, the foliage rolls around the edge to complete the carving, so that, in effect, the carving is almost in the round.

13-16 shows the side foliage carved into the edge of the band-sawed pattern without the edge form being altered in any way. It is still square and unnatural (for foliage). It is more difficult to carve as well, because of this unnatural shape, and certainly not easy to achieve a free flow of any kind. 13-17 shows a spray of leaves carved into a convex surface, rising up from a "base" that is the top of the rabbet for the mirror frame. The fish, complete with air bubbles, looks quite at home. The carving is easier to do, it looks much more natural, and the end result is therefore more pleasing.

THE CANDLESTICK MAKER

Carving on Turning

Carving on turning is a largely unexplored activity among the woodworking fraternity. Turners tend not to be carvers and carvers tend to stick to themselves. Combining the skills, however, can produce some very attractive results. It is to the carver's advantage, whether or not he or she wants to take up turning, to be able to instruct the turner to prepare "blanks" for carving, and to be able to choose designs that are appropriate for placing on turned wood. We also need to be able to transfer designs from the "flat" to the "round," prepare jigs to hold "round" objects, and choose and sharpen tools so that we can easily cut across the end grain.

This is our first truly "in-the-round" carving, although it does not have the visualization challenges that a less geometric carving would have.

It is important that instructions for the wood turner are clear and complete. Ideally, a template should be supplied to the turner with measurements included. 14-1 shows an original sketch, 14-2 and 14-3 profile template patterns, and 14-4 the turned billets ready for carving. At the top end of the candlestick a hole is bored for the candle. Some wood turners have the required machine change parts, so include instructions for this too.

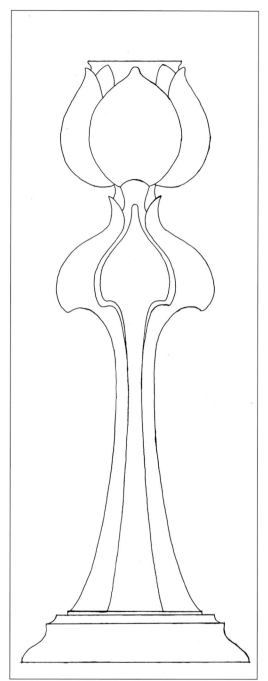

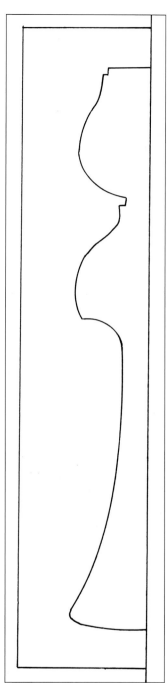

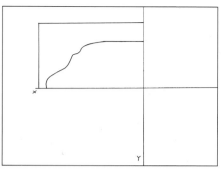

14-3. This is the profile template for the base. Make your dimensions to suit your circumstances. In the following examples, the spindle is 13¾ in (350mm) long and 3⅛ in (80mm) in diameter, its base is 4½ in (140mm) diameter, and it is 1⅛ in (30mm) thick.

14-1. From this initial drawing, make profile templates for your wood turner—such as those shown in 14-2 for the main profile and in 14-3 for the base. Leave nothing to chance or you may be surprised; specify how you want the base to be shaped, include instructions for the hole that you want bored in the top end of the candlestick—even specify the surface finish.

14-2. If you want more than "one off," a template is essential to help remove potential for error. Make it out of stiff cardboard or thin wood. Your turner will hold the profile against the turning, so make sure there is sufficient area to hold it comfortably.

14-4. Notice the turned billet is not the same as the drawing. The second bulb is quite different. The carver will be able to make it the same, but it is a lot easier if the template is correct in the first place. And as for the base? This is what can happen if there is no template. Say the turner decided he didn't like the drawing, and as a template was supplied for the spindle and not the base, he concluded: the base could be anything.

If you are to use your own boring equipment for the hole in the base, it is important that the turner make the peg on the end of the spindle the same diameter, otherwise you will not have decent glue-surface contact. The best thing to do is to supply the turner with a scrap of thin wood ¼ in (6mm) with a sample of the hole bored in it from your drill bit. This is the turner's template for the peg diameter, and removes margin for measuring error, or replaces a worn or even an eccentric boring bit. A measurement on your drill bit does not necessarily mean it will cut a hole the same size.

You will also need to instruct the turner as to the surface finish you require. Because you will be carving the surface, there is no need for it to be sanded (the turner could use abrasive paper, shavings, or steel wool for this purpose). "Off the chisel" will save time and, if you are paying for it, money. You also run the risk of residual sanding grit's ruining your chisel.

Unless you supply your own wood, you are at the mercy of the turner for what you get, so you will need to take this into consideration too. The wood used in the examples shown in this chapter is Australian Huon pine.

If you have any doubts about your design and its appropriateness for turning, check with the turner before you proceed too far. A competent turner will be able to assist with design limitations.

Once you have your blank spindle, you will need to make a holding device. The simplest way to hold the spindle is shown in 14-5. The most important thing is that the spindle doesn't accidentally turn around while you are carving, otherwise you may damage the carving or yourself. In the jig shown there is a 4-in (100mm) wood screw in each end that can be tightened considerably. If necessary, you could place a wedge between the spindle and the base of the jig to stop it turning; however, be careful you don't damage the carving.

This jig is firmly clamped to the workbench with two C-clamps. Notice the clamps are at one end, so that the carving area is left unencumbered. Apart from being in the way of your hands, the clamps are a potential source of damage to the tools if they touch on them. Notice also that the end of the jig where the bulbs are is rounded off at about the same level and the same shape as the circumference of the spindle, allowing free access to the bulb for your carving tools.

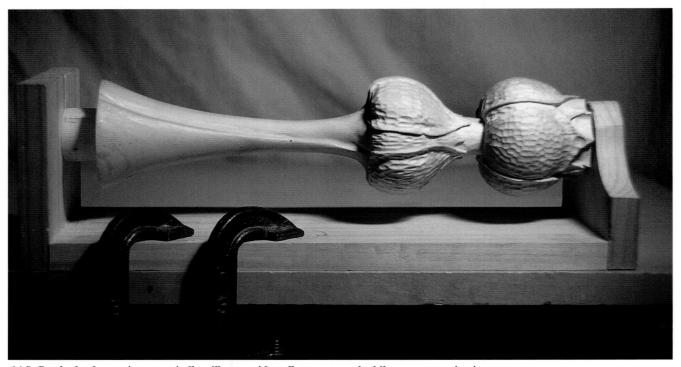

14-5. Be absolutely certain your spindle will not accidentally turn around while you are carving it.

Drawing the Pattern

One of the objectives with this carving is to "rework" the surface of the spindle to disguise the fact that it was turned in the first place. As we are to place the pattern around a circular shape, and as we are to carve a pattern that is uniform in its distribution of segments, we need to determine the way to place these segments equally around the spindle. This process of equal division is called "indexing." Once you have created the basic pattern and decided the number of segments it will have, divide the circle into equal parts and place the pattern accordingly.

Most modern wood-turning lathes have an indexing facility built in, so that your turner will be able to mark with a pencil as many equal divisions as you need. Most lathes with this facility will accommodate up to 24 divisions (15 degrees each), which are more than enough for this carving. If you are unable to have this done for you, you will need to do it manually. This task will require you to mark, in the first instance, divisions on the circumference at the end where the candle goes. This is the larger diameter of the two ends, and will be a lot easier to handle than the peg. Use a compass, protractor, or other drawing instrument to place the number of divisions you need for your pattern.

The pattern seen in 14-1 has four main petals, with four petal tips showing between them. There are therefore eight divisions required to be drawn on the pattern, with 45 degrees between each mark. You will need to make divisions on the second bulb equal to the first. Therefore, the divisions you make must be not only equal in degrees but directly above one another (i.e., in a straight line) from one end of the spindle to the other. Do not try to accomplish this freehand, unless you are very skilled at it, because you will likely not get everything in line, as is the case in 14-6. The red line at the top of the frame marks the center of the spindle. One of the petal tips (between two major petals) coincides with this mark. The carver marked in freehand in gray pencil a centerline all the way to the peg on the other end. When the spindle was actually mounted in the jig and the corresponding center mark to the top was made at the bottom (the red line on the bottom of the jig), you can clearly see the error made by the carver. There is about a ⅜-in (10mm) gap between the gray pencil line and the correct red line on the shoulder of the flair at the bottom end of the spindle.

14-6. Mark the divisions using a protractor or compass around the top of the spindle, mark a centerline at each end of the jig, and rotate the spindle, marking in each division on the second bulb, holding a rule between the centers on the jig.

Points to Consider as You Begin Carving

✳ Ensure accurate indexing, and sketch on one petal first. Visually assess that the others will fit before drawing them onto the wood.

✳ Use a soft pencil that will not indent the surface, in case you need to erase the lines.

✳ Make sure you overlap the petals in the right order, and place a stop-cut along the lines of the petals.

✳ As with previous carvings, if you wish to decorate the surface as has been done in these, it is best to get the shape of the petals organized before you decorate them. Not only are the petals focal areas in this carving, so are the junctions at the top.

✳ Make sure you achieve clean shadows in these areas.

14-7

14-8

The easiest procedure is to mount the spindle in the jig and, with the centers marked on the jig, use a steel rule to position the centerline along key parts of the spindle. The steel rule is flexible and bends over the second bulb. As you have marked the top of the spindle with the required divisions, it is just a matter of rotating the spindle and placing in position the remaining locations for the petal tips.

One finished pattern is shown earlier on page 138 in 14-5. In the top bulb, the four petals are set out so that two of them are overlapped by the other two, and in the bottom bulb the four petals are smaller, such that the "underneath" petals are exposed (in the top bulb only the tips of these are showing). You can imagine the non-alignment that would occur if the indexing were not correct.

The sequence of the carving is shown in 14-7, 14-8, 14-9, and 14-10. Mark out all the petals first, as shown in 14-7, and then separate them with a stop-cut, which you can just see in 14-8, and separate out the in-between tips. You can also see in 14-7 and 14-8 the wood turner's gouge scuff marks on the circumference of the top bulb—this is what is meant by "off the chisel." 14-8 shows that the right-hand petal will overlap the left—and 14-9 shows the overlap on the other side of the same petal. 14-10 shows 14-8 carved.

14-9

14-10

Now look at 14-11, which is the close-up of 14-10. There are two things in particular to consider. First, from a design point of view, the junction of the petals could be a lot clearer or better defined. At the junction the petal corners are almost at the same plane, so we need to give more depth to the separation. This you will see completed in 14-12. Notice how much stronger the shadow is between the petals under the same lighting?

The other thing to notice in 14-11 is the chip of wood that has been glued back into the edge of the petal just to the above right of the petal junction. Unless something is done with it, it will be a very obvious repair job. 14-13 shows what can be done to hide it and, with a little abrasive paper to smooth it over, it will be almost invisible under normal viewing conditions. Use glue that dries clear—an acrylic copolymer was used in this instance—then make a paste with some sanding dust from a scrap of the same species. This is then used as filler, and the patch is hidden.

Having made the shadow stronger between the petals, the carver then decided that the curvature of the petal around its perimeter wasn't deep enough, so it was redone (see 14-14). The trouble is that this activity re-exposed the chip, which is now very clearly visible to the above right of the petal junction, and the filling process had to be repeated. This is a good example of how one alteration can lead to a chain reaction, and while it is not always that easy to avoid (except in hindsight!), it demonstrates the need to thoroughly think things through to minimize the possibility of further and worse damage being done. The final repair and re-carve with stronger overall shadows is shown in 14-15, before any surface finishing, which in this case will be a very touch-off with 600-grit aluminum oxide paper, then a neutral-colored surface sealer and a light coat of wax.

A similar pattern being carved quite differently is shown in 14-16. It is always amazing what a difference can be achieved using precisely the same outline but a different surface curve. Neither one is necessarily better or worse, they are simply different. In this example, the lines and curves are softer, the shadows weaker, with nonetheless a very pleasant outcome.

14-11

14-12

14-13. The repair is well disguised by sanding powder in the glue.

14-15. Almost invisible now, this repair will never be noticed.

14-14. Unfortunately the chip is exposed again, risking the need for further repair when the petal is re-carved.

14-16. More of an "onion" motif—this is a quite effective design.

The pattern seen in 14-17 is similar to 14-15, with the curl around the edge of the petal more acute. Notice the stringy surface in the troughs? This is a characteristic of Huon pine when combined with a tool that may not be sharp enough or may be ground with the wrong bevel shape for the wood. Huon pine likes a thin bevel and an ultra-sharp edge, although in these troughs you could experiment with a slightly rounder bevel, provided it doesn't get too thick at the cutting edge. In this particular example, it became evident, however, that the jig was the main offender. The corners of the support upright bracket had not been cut off as they are in 14-17, so that they limited the access of the tool to the wood, making it difficult for the carver to approach the wood without chipping and tearing at it.

At the base of each bulb, and in particular with the lower one, which in 14-18 can be seen to have been turned slightly concave, it becomes necessary to carve across the end grain.

End-grain carving is particularly useful for wood-block printing or mold making when the design requires no wood-grain pattern to be visible, or when a particularly fine engraving is required that can only be achieved in end grain. Some species respond very well to end-grain carving, such as stone fruit woods and boxwood, but many are also unsuitable because they tend to "squash" rather than cut. Monterey pine, Malaysian kauri, and Western red cedar provide good demonstrations of this. The one thing that is essential is a sharp tool, otherwise compression rather than cutting will almost certainly be the result.

In the case of our candlestick, access is also difficult to the base of the bulb, so you are encouraged to try a reverse bent tool (refer to Chapter 2, "Which Tool?") for shaping these underparts. Don't thin the bevel too much, because these tools require some (but very little) roundness of the bevel to work well, and do make sure it is very keenly honed. If the fibers and cells in the end grain do collapse when they are

14-18. If you wish to carve underneath the bulb, this will require skill with end-grain carving. A very sharp reverse bent tool may give best results in this configuration.

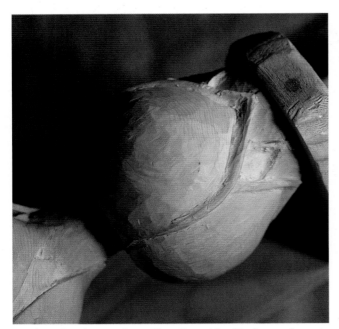

14-17. This stringy surface will need considerable time to clean up.

carved, sometimes they will break below the surface, which makes repairing very difficult. A sharp tool is the most effective way to prevent this. If you use a mallet, be reasonably gentle with it, otherwise it might do more harm than good.

The base of the candlestick need not be carved; however, you will notice in 14-20 that some light relief enhances the finished work. A clear sealer and wax can be used once again as an effective surface finish. Huon pine does have a natural waxy content, so that wax applied directly to it can also give a very pleasing result.

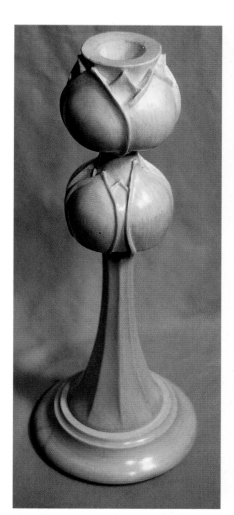

14-19. This is the candlestick in 14-17 and 14-18 after cleaning up. The acute rise on the edge of the petals is quite effective. The fluted pedestal is very acceptable.

14-20. A four-sided pedestal and substantially different top and bottom bulbs give strong shadows. Note that the base has a simple foliage design.

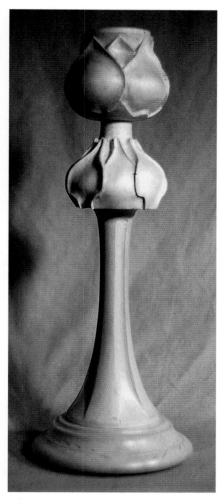

14-21. The eight segments of the pedestal, alternately high and low, are very pleasant. Note that the stronger shadows on the bottom bulb appear out of balance with those on the top bulb.

chapter 15

A COAT OF ARMS

Heraldry

For proficiency as a decorative woodcarver, we need to be able to carve for the present and prepare for the future. In this chapter, we will put all our skills to the test, from our very own interpretation of design to selecting the best wood for our purposes. We will make a coat of arms that can be dismantled at a later date for renovation—hopefully after we have long since departed!

To create our carving so that it can be literally pulled apart for easy repair and renovation, we will need to be able to choose and design the separate components, and decide how we will join them together. We will need to decide on surface coatings or whether to use different-colored species for effect.

From concept, to design, to creation, to repair. That just about completes the cycle. And if the creation is representative and symbolic of a part of our lives, as is a coat of arms, then all the better. Woodcarving is a tradition, has a tradition, and above all, as an art form, will continue to develop tradition.

The symbolism that became heraldry is a very important part of our everyday lives. Whether one considers it an art or a science, there always remains the stirring of emotions representing pride, power, fear, ownership, or membership. Whether personal, national, or international, symbolism has a major influence on many decisions individuals and communities make.

It is to be expected, then, that such symbolism will in many respects be a language unto itself. As such, it will be no surprise that at some point in time there will be a specific symbol for a specific representation; and the use of incorrect symbolism may well be considered insulting or, at the very least, an unfortunate display of ignorance.

To this end, it is important that the creation of symbolism be well researched, particularly if it is to be passed off as representing a meaningful communication or statement.

For the three projects we discuss in this chapter, no commentary is made about the legitimacy of each crest for any particular purpose, nor are there any assumptions with regard to the accuracy or otherwise of the crests as heraldic statements, nor will we use heraldic "language."

The Brief

For each crest, there are common characteristics that must be considered. These characteristics include future renovation, the surface finish, the weight of the piece, and the stability of the wood over a long period of time. The considerations are outlined in the box below.

Considerations for Each Crest

Renovation

✳ The crest must be made in such a way that it can be easily renovated. The reason for this is simply that crests are often complex structures, and if a component is damaged there needs to be an easy operation to replace it without disruption to other parts.

✳ It will be necessary to identify which parts of the design should and can be made as separate pieces, and we will decide how best to hold the pieces together when completed.

Surface Finish

✳ Surface finish may also affect renovation, especially if you use an obscure one that won't be easy to replace or one that deteriorates quickly.

✳ The choice of finish may also affect the way in which the carving is done, for example in the case of gilding.

✳ If the crest is to be mounted in an out-of-the-way place that cannot be easily accessed, then you won't want to use oil finishes that look "off" after only a short time, or waxes that need constant replenishing.

✳ If you choose a natural wood look, then you may need to use ultraviolet-light filters on the surface to help maintain the wood color.

Weight

✳ Weight is a major consideration if your crest is to be mounted on a wall, for example. You will need to know the wall construction method and decide the most appropriate affixing system.

✳ If there is any doubt as to the strength of this system, then you will need to ensure the woods you use are not so dense as to make wall mounting dangerous.

Wood Stability

✳ As the crest is to be in place for some time, it will be necessary to ensure that the wood you use is stable, and will not check or otherwise wind, cup, or warp. Being correctly seasoned for the environment is a paramount requirement.

✳ Avoid placing the carving in an environment where it will be exposed to direct sunlight, and don't use high-moisture-content wood and place it in a dry air-conditioned area.

15-1. A version of the coat of arms of Finland.

15-2. The black-and-white enlargement used for cutting out patterns.

Example 1

Design and Construction

The pattern for this crest, shown in 15-1, was derived from a pamphlet of unknown origin. It is thought to be a rendition of the coat of arms of Finland.

The shield will be 17¾ in (450mm) high, painted with oil gloss enamel, and mounted on a wall in a house. The carved parts are minimal in size and therefore weight, so there should be few, if any, stability problems. The shield therefore does not need to hold any great mass and can be of lightweight construction.

It was decided to construct the shield from medium-density fiberboard and use jelutong for the carved lion components and the rosettes.

From the color version in 15-1, scanning and enlarging to actual size created

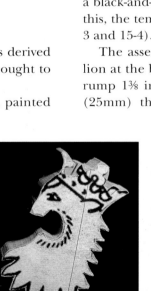

15-3. The lion's head in the making.

a black-and-white working drawing. This is 15-2. From this, the templates were cut to make the parts (see 15-3 and 15-4).

The assessment of the design concluded that the lion at the beard would be 2 in (50mm) thick, at the rump 1⅜ in (35mm) thick, the right hind leg 1 in (25mm) thick, the tail and swords ½ in (13mm) thick, and the rosettes ¼ in (6mm).

It was also decided that the shield would be "stepped" at the perimeter, and a white stripe would be added around the border, so that the red part of the shield would be sitting on top of a thinner piece that formed the border. This can be seen in 15-5.

Jelutong sealed with oil-based paint makes for a very stable carving, and this had a significant impact on the choice of system for holding the components together. Rather than using screws, it was decided to pin each component with a ⅛-in (3mm) dowel pierced into the back of the component by a minimum of ³⁄₁₆ in (4mm), and then through both shield components. Therefore, the same pins that held the components in place would hold the shield pieces together as well. For repair work, it would be a simple matter of pulling the piece off, repairing, and then pressing it back onto the dowel.

This system would be unsatisfactory for anything other than a very stable carving, because any movement in the wood will make the pieces loose. Particularly in a stable home environment, this method should be perfectly satisfactory.

Compared to some of the previous exercises in other chapters, the carving itself is not all that difficult. It is the combination of this simplicity of design with the three colors applied that makes it attractive. It is clean, uncluttered, bright, and very eye-catching.

The method used for transferring the patterns ready for scroll sawing are shown in 15-3, and some of the components during carving are seen in 15-4. You will notice on the sword and the leg the sap pockets that are so typical of jelutong. These will need to be filled with putty before undercoating. Use only shrink-free putty in these circumstances, as there will be nothing worse than hollows appearing in the gloss paint work! You may also need to check that the putty does not suck moisture from the paint, which may cause a blemish that might be visible in the finished work. If you have any doubt, test it in a hole on a scrap and paint it at least with the undercoat.

The actual carving on each component has no fine detail that will be hidden when coated with undercoat and two or three topcoats of paint, so there is no special need to carve in a way that makes allowances for

15-5. The finished parts before assembly. They will be pinned with thin dowel. Do not use this technique unless the parts are thoroughly sealed and will not "move"; otherwise they will eventually fall off.

this. If this had been necessary, deeper cuts may have been required in some places.

An "exploded" view of the crest is shown in 15-5, the simplicity of the "dissection" being obvious.

The completed crest can be seen in 15-6—in all, a neat, tidy, and effective package with no complicating factors.

15-4. Separate components before painting. It is essential to constantly check that all the parts fit neatly together.

15-6. The carved version of the coat of arms of Finland.

Example 2

Design and Construction

This family crest was made from a set of drawings, some of which are shown in 15-7. The crest is to be 12 in (300mm) in diameter, with the deepest part, the buckle, 2 in (50mm) thick. It will be painted with an acrylic silver finish.

It was decided that the circle would be made in four parts and mounted on a backboard and painted. The circle would be joined each side of the buckle and each end of the motto. A butt join would be used in each case, and each component screwed in place.

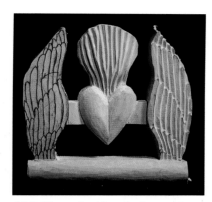

15-8. The center piece during carving.

It was decided that, for stability and light weight, jelutong would again be used for the carved components, and ¼-in (6mm) thick medium-density fiberboard for the back plate.

The centerpiece, motto, and buckle during the carving process are shown in 15-8, 15-9, and 15-10.

There is a reasonable degree of difficulty with the motto in this crest, as well as with the grooves in the remainder of the "belt." The reason for this is the awkwardness in gaining access to the letters on the one hand and the background of the belt on the other. These are ideal situations for short, bent gouges.

You will notice in the lettering shown in 15-9 that there is variation in the thickness of the parts of the letters, particularly noticeable, for example, in the "O" in "LUGEO." This is unfortunate, as the motto is a definite focal point of a crest, and a critical eye will most likely notice this straight away. There is no easier solution to this challenge than practice. From a design point of view, there are two things that could be considered that would make carving them easier, and they are:

✳ Lower the border to the same height as the letters. This would not detract from the design.

✳ Make the letters thicker, which will have the visual effect of making very small variations a little less obvious. They will not "disappear," but they will be less noticeable.

15-7. Various drawings and a lettering template for a family crest. It is always best to make a set of drawings of actual size. Scale drawings can be cumbersome to use, take too much time to draw, and create another step that can allow error to be introduced.

15-9. The motto during carving. Be careful to get the letters uniform.

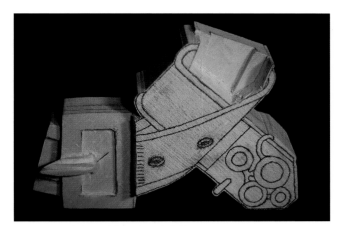

15-10. The belt buckle before finishing.

A weakness in the carving construction is the tongue of the buckle that goes through the belt. The grain direction is along the tongue, making it weak in cross section. In fact, it was bumped and broken during carving, and had to be renovated (glued up) before it was finished! Unfortunately, that was not all. In the previous example, we discussed the stability of the carved components once they are sealed with oil-based paint. With this crest, a stability problem occurred causing the butt joins to open, one of which is shown in 15-11. There is speculation as to the cause of this, one of which is the use of acrylic paint, which can have some porous characteristics that allow moisture to come and go from the wood. This is most likely not the case with this example; however, it is worth noting that potentially there is a doubt as to the efficacy of acrylic paint as a total sealer from moisture. Oil-based paints are a much safer proposition in the regard. If your carving is to be gilded with gold leaf and it is made from laminated blocks that may start to de-laminate (if subjected to varying ambient moisture levels), it is wise, for the same reasons, to consider the oil gilding method rather than the water gilding method.

The most likely explanation for the opening of the joints is that they were not glued together, which was a conscious decision because of the nature of the requirement that the carving be able to be dismantled. This requirement, therefore, made it more imperative that there be "built-in" stability.

You will note, from 15-12, that the back of the crest is not sealed. The material used is a compacted reconstituted wood-fiber product that will move a little under varying moisture conditions. A period of continuous wet weather most likely caused expansion of the backboard, forcing the joints open. The joints stayed open for several days; however, after another period of continuous dry weather, they closed up and were almost invisible.

It is imperative that all surfaces are properly sealed. Just because they are out of sight doesn't mean they will stay out of mind! The finished crest is shown in 15-13.

15-11. Movement in joints is very unfortunate. Every precaution should be taken to avoid this happening.

15-12. The unsealed back of the crest, showing locations of the joints for a future renovator. These notations can be very useful. Unfortunately, the first renovator was the maker!

15-13. The finished family crest.

Example 3

Design and Construction

The following crest is a somewhat more complex arrangement. The pencil drawing in 15-14 shows a large number of components that will need some careful planning to separate them. The carving itself is also more complex than the previous examples, although it is representative of work achieved in the prior chapters. We can see in 15-15 the manner in which the components were separated, and 15-16, 15-17, 15-18, 15-19, 15-20, 15-21, and 15-22 show close-up views of some of these components and first and second goes.

The soldier's hand and the top of the helmet have holes drilled in them to accommodate the lance shafts, and the soldier's feet are pinned with metal pins (nails) that fit into small holes also in the helmet.

Notice that the carving of the soldier is in essence childlike. The proportions of the arms and legs, and the shape and detail of the face in particular. For a first effort in this kind of work, it is, however, very creditable. Without any doubt, the human form is particularly difficult to "get right" first go. The shapes are complex, and to achieve realism takes considerable effort and practice. Whatever you do, if you attempt a human form and don't like it first time round, never give up—always have another go. It is rare that the first attempt will be perfect; however, it is also very common for the learning curve to be quite fast, so chances are your second attempt will be amazingly improved.

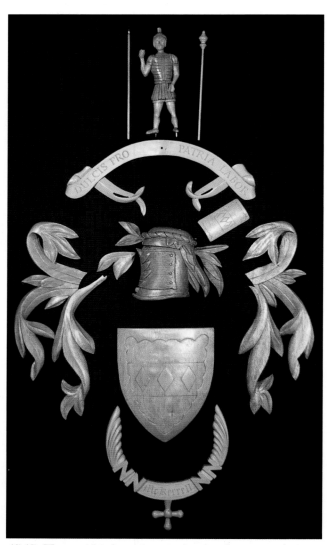

15-15. The completed components showing the manner in which they were separated.

15-14. A more complex, full-sized drawing, 29½ in × 21¾ in (750mm × 550mm), of another family crest.

15-16. The soldier and lances during carving.

This "redoing" of all or part of your unsatisfactory work is particularly important. If you are attentive to always doing your best to improve your observation skills and translate what you are looking at into a more realistic end result, your labors will indeed be well rewarded.

A case in point is the foliage for this crest, one piece of which the carver did twice for a significant improvement to the end result. The rejected component can be seen in 15-19 and the second attempt is shown in 15-20. The main offender is the top portion of the sprig, which should sit above the remainder. Can you see the shadow line in 15-20 that separates the top leaf from those hanging below it? It has been carved the opposite way in the rejected original in 15-19. This is raw wood, which is why it is a different color from the final piece in 15-20, which is actually the same species (white meranti) finished with a polyurethane coating.

15-17. The helmet of red meranti during carving.

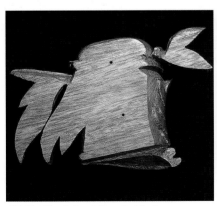

15-18. The helmet from behind.

15-19. This was the first attempt to carve the foliage that is shown in 15-20. The shadow lines needed rearrangement.

15-20. Folioage of white beech during carving, second attempt; finished with a polyurethane coating.

15-21. One of the components during carving.

The finish for this carving is very important. The maker decided to leave it as a natural-wood coat of arms, with no coloring added, except to the soldier (and there was no real reason for coloring this). The great danger with leaving things natural is that constant exposure to ultraviolet light will eventually change the color of the different species and destroy the color differences that have been set up. It is imperative, therefore, that several coatings be applied of a surface finish that includes an effective long-term ultraviolet-light filter. It is also important that nothing be placed over the top of this coating, so that additional applications may be applied to ensure the longevity of the filter system. Under no circumstances should a wax be applied.

Each of the components was screwed to the shield made from 10-ply, which was surface-treated with a faint lime wash to give a little more color contrast to the carved components. The finished crest is shown in 15-23.

The helmet is made from red meranti (one of the meranti subspecies), the foliage, soldier, and center shield from white meranti, and the remainder from white beech.

15-23. The finished crest sealed with a satin polyurethane finish with added ultraviolet filter.

15-22. One of the components during carving.

Example 4

Design and Construction

This family crest stands a meter high and 16 in (400mm) wide, and is set on a background of this Scottish family's tartan. 15-24 shows the motto, hand, and sword in progress, with the outline of the remainder in pencil on the backing board, which is medium-density fiberboard. All the components are shown in "exploded" form in 15-25.

The finished crest can be seen in 15-26. There are interesting design issues with this crest that are best explained with reference to the assembled and finished crest. You will want to refer to 15-26 for the discussion of these issues on the next page.

15-25. Each of the very accurately cut pieces will fit snugly into one another in a neat, uncomplicated arrangement.

15-24. Fitting components to a full-sized drawing on the backing board is a good method to ensure easy assembly. In the final work, four screws set in from the back are all that are needed to hold this crest together.

15-26. The assembled crest, a relatively simple yet powerful design.

The motto, made from Honduras mahogany, is butt jointed from three sections with the cell direction running the length of each of the curved components. This is done to reduce the potential for the ribbon on which the motto is carved to twist.

You will note the letters "AUT" are carved into wood that is a different color from the other two sections of the ribbon. Color variation is often difficult to avoid, particularly if the components are cut from different stock; however, less variation than this would have improved the overall result.

15-27. The blotches on the bear's face are a characteristic of kauri when it is carved, and it will take some patience to remove them.

15-28. Clean lettering is very achievable in Honduras mahogany.

The tip of the sword projects beyond the boundary of the tartan background. This was intentional by the maker, and it is a matter of design preference by the individual observer. Our minds tend to think everything should be "framed," so this design element would normally be considered "different." Which, of course, is not to say it is "bad."

The helmet, in South American walnut, is a little dark for balance and contrast with the background. A light color, or one with some striation of a lighter color in it, may have created a more pleasing effect. African mahogany may have been a better choice, as it has a lighter color striped through it.

The shield is carved in kauri, one of the very stringy woods on which it is very hard to achieve an evenly smooth surface finish. If you look at 15-27, you will see a blotchy appearance on the bear's face. Some of this is a result of shadows caused by tool marks that have not yet been removed, and some by the torn end of the cells right on the surface of the wood. This apparent discoloration is a result of the torn surface (it is still very fine but nevertheless "torn") reflecting a light "duller" than the remainder of the surface. To remove this blotchy look, it is necessary to very finely carve the surface with an ultra-sharp tool, then use a surface hardener such as white shellac before final waxing with a clear wax. A gray wax will discolor the carving.

A closer view of the lettering on the motto is shown in 15-28. The lettering is very cleanly cut, although there is still some double image in the bottoms of the "V"s. Notice the sanding dust in the groove around the circumference?

As we have said, kauri is generally very difficult to carve. In 15-29 the top edges of the flags have sustained some chipping, especially noticeable on the top edge of the middle flag.

The carving (apart from the shield described above) is finished with 1000-grit paper, then with orange oil and a clear wax. If you compare the richness of the color of the wood in 15-30 with the more bland color of the wood in 15-29 (they are lit the same way photographically), you can very readily accept the impact that finishing has on the end product. If you have any doubts at all about your planned end result, be sure to take the safe route and test it on off-cuts first.

The overall effect of this crest is very good, and the standard of work very impressive for a person who has just begun the carving journey.

15-29. *Chipping on the edges is also a characteristic of kauri. It requires thin, beveled, very sharp tools to help avoid this.*

15-30. *Rich color is achieved with the use of oil finishes, in this case orange oil.*

APPENDIX

Common and Botanical Names of Wood

Cultivated in the United States and Canada

ALDER (Black)	*Alnus glutinosa*
APPLE (Crab)	*Malus sylvestris*
ASH (European)	*Fraxinus exelsior*
(Mountain)	*Eucalyptus regnans*
(White)	*Fraxinus americana*
BALSA	*Ochroma pyramidale*
BASSWOOD	*Tilia* spp. (see Linden)
BEECH (American)	*Fagus grandifolia*
(European)	*Fagus sylvatica*
(White)	*Gmelina leichardtii*
BOX (Brisbane)	*Tristania conferta*
BOXWOOD	*Buxus sempervirens*
CAMPHOR TREE	*Cinnamomum camphora*
CEDAR (Western red)	*Thuja plicata*
CHERRY (Black, Wild)	*Prunus serotina*
CHESTNUT (European)	*Castanea sativa*
CYPRESS	*Cupressus* spp.
DEVIL TREE (Cheesewood)	*Alstonia scholaris*
DOGWOOD	*Cornus* spp.
DOUGLAS FIR	*Pseudotsuga menziesii*
EBONY	*Diospyros ebenum*
GUM (Scribbly)	*Eucalyptus haemastoma*
HICKORY	*Carya* spp.
KAURI	*Agathis* spp.
LINDEN (Lime)	*Tilia* spp.
OAK	*Quercus* spp.
(Cork)	*Quercus suber*
PADAUK	*Pterocarpus indicus*
PEAR (Common)	*Pyrus communis*
PINE (Huon)	*Dacrydium franklinii*
(Monterey)	*Pinus radiata*
POPLAR (White)	*Populus alba*
RED BLOODWOOD	*Eucalyptus gumnifera*
REDWOOD	*Sequoia sempervirens*
RIMU	*Dacrydiurn cupressinum*
SANDALWOOD	*Santalum album*
SYCAMORE (American)	*Platanus occidentalis*
TALLOWWOOD (White)	*Eucalyptus microcorys*
TOTARA	*Podocarpus totara*
WALNUT	*Juglans* spp.
WEEPING MYALL	*Acacia pendula*
WENGE	*Millettia* spp.
WILLOW	*Salix* spp.
YEW	*Taxus baccata*

Imported

BLACK BEAN (Australian)	*Dyera costulata*
BOLLYWOOD	*Litsea reticulata*
JARRAH	*Eucalyptus marginata*
JELUTONG	*Dyera costulata*
LIGNUMVITAE	*Guaiacum officinale*
MAHOGANY (Honduras)	*Swietana macrophylla*
MERANTI (Lauan)	*Shorea* spp.
MERBAU (Kwila)	*Intsia bijuga*
PURPLEHEART	*Peltogyne* spp.
TEAK	*Tectona grandis*
WATTLE (Australian gidgee)	*Acacia cambegei*

Metric Equivalents

inches	mm	cm
1/8	3	0.3
1/4	6	0.6
3/8	10	1.0
1/2	13	1.3
5/8	16	1.6
3/4	19	1.9
7/8	22	2.2
1	25	2.5
1 1/4	32	3.2
1 1/2	38	3.8
1 3/4	44	4.4
2	51	5.1
2 1/2	64	6.4

inches	mm	cm	inches	mm	cm
3	76	7.6	13	330	33.0
3 1/2	89	8.9	14	356	35.6
4	102	10.2	15	381	38.1
4 1/2	114	11.4	16	406	40.6
5	127	12.7	17	432	43.2
6	152	15.2	18	457	45.7
7	178	17.8	19	483	48.3
8	203	20.3	20	508	50.8
9	229	22.9	21	533	53.3
10	254	25.4	22	559	55.9
11	279	27.9	23	584	58.4
12	305	30.5	24	610	61.0

Conversions

1 inch = 25.4 mm   1 mm = 0.039 inch   mm = millimeter
1 foot = 304.8 mm   1 m = 3.28 feet   cm = centimeter
   m = meter

INDEX